A guide to
Knitting

igloobooks.com

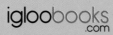

Published in 2012
by Igloo Books Ltd
Cottage Farm
Sywell
NN6 0BJ
www.igloobooks.com

Copyright© 2012 Igloo Books Ltd

All projects, content and images supplied by Handmade Living Magazine

CTP001 0812
2 4 6 8 10 9 7 5 3 1
ISBN 978-0-85780-664-2

Printed and manufactured in China

A guide to
Knitting

Contents

Introduction

Follow the step-by-step instructions in this comprehensive how-to guide and learn to fashion your own garments and accessories using basic stitches and a drop of creativity.

LEARN TO KNIT:
The Basic Stitches

The following pages contain the basic stitches that you will need to begin knitting. Each how-to section covers a different stitch, with comprehensive step-by-step explanation and accompanying images.

Slipknot

Step 1
A slipknot is the first stage of any cast on. Loop the yarn around two fingers of the left hand, the ball end on top. Dip the needle into the loop, catch the ball end of the yarn and pull it through the loop.

Step 2
Pull the ends of the yarn to tighten the knot. Tighten the ball end to bring the knot up to the needle.

Ends
The end of yarn left after casting on should be a reasonable length of approx 10-30cm/4-12in so that it can be used for sewing up. The same applies to the end left after casting off.

Long-tail Cast On

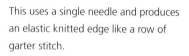

This uses a single needle and produces an elastic knitted edge like a row of garter stitch.

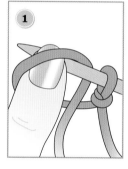

Step 1
Leaving an end about three times the length of the required cast-on, put a slipknot on the needle. Holding the yarn end in the left hand, take the left thumb under the yarn and upwards. Insert the needle in the loop just made on the thumb.

Step 2
Use the ball end of the yarn to make a knit stitch, slipping the loop off the thumb. Pull the yarn end to close the stitch up to the needle. Continue making stitches in this way.

Chain Cast Off

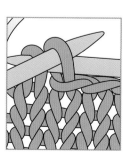

A simple knit stitch cast off is used in most of these projects. Knit two stitches. * With the left needle, lift the first stitch over the second. Knit the next stitch. Repeat from * until one stitch remains. Break the yarn, take the end through this stitch and tighten.

Knit Stitch (K)

Purl Stitch (P)

Choose to hold the yarn and needles in whichever way you feel most comfortable. To create tension in the yarn – that is, to keep it moving evenly – you will need to twist it through some fingers of the hand holding the yarn, and maybe even take it around your little finger. Continuous rows of knit stitch produce garter stitch. It does take some practice to get the stitches even so don't be discouraged, keep on practising.

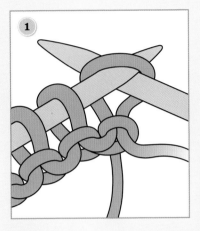

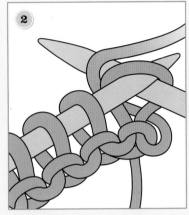

Step 1
Insert the right needle into the first stitch on the left needle. Make sure it goes from left to right into the front of the stitch.

Step 2
Taking the yarn behind, bring it up and around the right needle.

Step 3
Using the tip of the right needle, draw a loop of yarn through the stitch.

Step 4
Slip the stitch off the left needle. There is now a new stitch on the right needle.

Step 1
Insert the right needle into the first stitch on the left needle. Make sure it goes into the stitch from right to left.

Step 2
Lower the tip of the right needle, taking it away from you to draw a loop of yarn through the stitch.

Step 3
Taking the yarn to the front, loop it around the right needle.

Step 4
Slip the stitch off the left needle. There is now a new stitch on the right needle.

Decreases

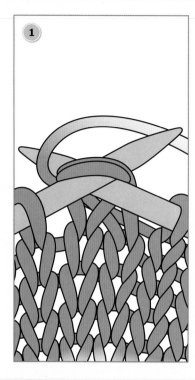

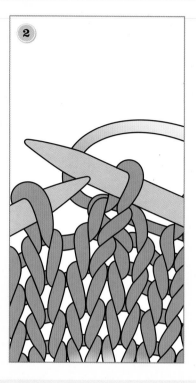

Decreases have two basic functions. They can be used to reduce the number of stitches in a row, as in armholes and necklines, and combined with increases, they can create stitch patterns.

Right-slanting single decrease (k2tog)

Knitting two stitches together makes a smooth shaping, with the second stitch lying on top of the first.

Step 1

Insert the right needle through the front of the first two stitches on the left needle, then take the yarn around the needle.

Step 2

Draw the loop through and drop the two stitches off the left needle.

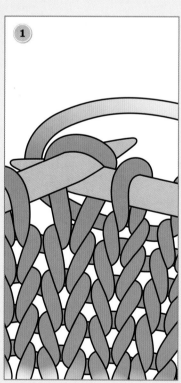

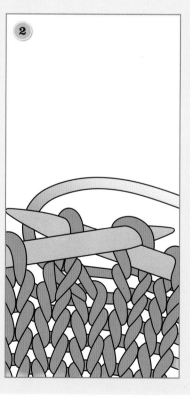

Left-slanting double decrease (sk2po)

For a double decrease that slants to the left, worked on a right-side row, you'll need to take the first stitch over a single decrease. For a similar-looking decrease worked on a wrong-side row, purl three together through the back of the loops (p3tog tbl).

Step 1

Insert the right needle knitwise through the front of the first stitch on the left needle, and slip it onto the right needle.

Step 2

Knit the next two stitches together, then lift the first stitch over as shown. To make a right-slanting double decrease, simply knit three stitches together (k3tog).

Cables

Knitting groups of stitches out of sequence creates exciting stitch patterns. Cables can be worked with two or more stitches and crossed to the front or the back.

Front cable (c4f)

The stitches in this example are knitted, and this four-stitch cable crosses at the front. A four-stitch back cable (c4b) is worked in exactly the same way, except that the cable needle is held at the back, so that the cable crosses in the opposite direction.

Step 1

Slip the first two stitches onto a cable needle and hold at the front of the work, then knit the next two stitches from the left needle.

Step 2

Knit the two stitches from the cable needle.

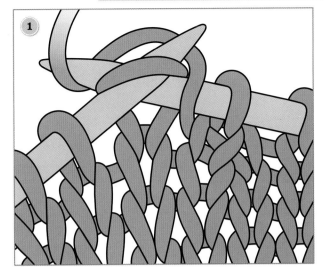

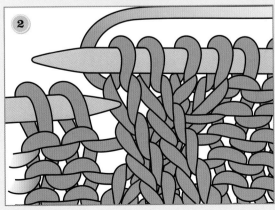

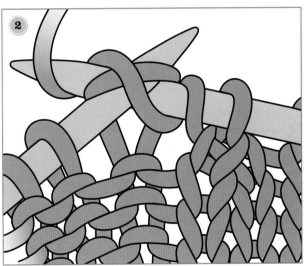

Yarn Over (YO)

It's essential to take the yarn over the needle so that the strand lies in the same direction as the other stitches. Working into this strand on the next row makes a hole, but if the strand is twisted, the hole will close up. When the stitch before a yarn over is purl, the yarn will already be at the front, ready to go over the needle.

Step 1

To make a yarn over between knit stitches, bring the yarn to the front as if to purl, then take it over the needle to knit the next stitch.

Step 2

To make a yarn over between a knit and a purl, bring the yarn to the front as if to purl, take it over the needle and bring it to the front again, ready to purl.

11

Increases

Here are two of the most basic methods of increasing a single stitch – bar increase and lifted strand increase.

Bar increase on a knit row (kfb)

Knitting into the front and the back of a stitch is the most common increase. It's a neat, firm increase, which makes a little bar on the right side of the work at the base of the new stitch. This makes it easy to count rows between shapings and doesn't leave a hole.

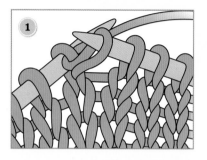 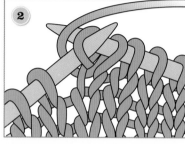 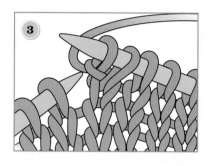

Step 1

Knit into the front of the stitch and pull the loop through, but leave the stitch on the left needle.

Step 2

Knit into the back of the stitch on the left needle.

Step 3

Slip the stitch off the left needle, making two stitches on the right needle. Note that the bar of the new stitch lies on the left.

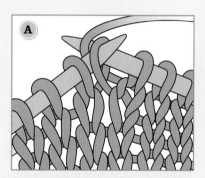 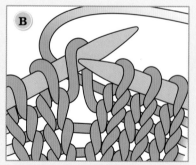 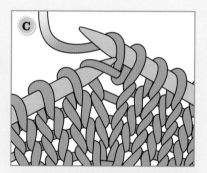

Lifted strand increase to the left (m1 or m1L)

Making a stitch from the strand between stitches is a very neat way to increase.

Picture A

From the front, insert the left needle under the strand between stitches. Make sure the strand lies on the needle in the same direction as the other stitches, then knit into the back of it.

Lifted strand increase to the right (m1R)

This right-slanting increase balances exactly the lifted strand increase to the left.

Picture B

From the back, insert the left needle under the strand between the stitches. It will not lie in the same direction as the other stitches, so knit into the front of it.

Double increase

This is one of the simplest ways to make three stitches out of one.

Picture C

Knit one stitch without slipping it off, take the yarn over the right needle from front to back then knit the same stitch again. A small but decorative hole is left in the fabric.

Twists

Twisting stitches is working two or three stitches out of sequence, but without using a cable needle.
This is an easy way to create patterns where lines of stitches travel over the surface of the knitting.

Left twist (t2L)

This twist is worked on a right-side row. As the stitches change place, the first stitch lies on top and
slants to the left, while the stitch behind is worked through the back of the loop.

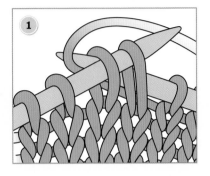 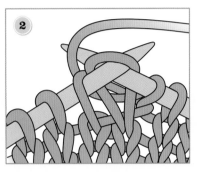 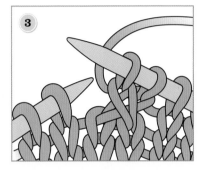

Step 1
Knit into the back of the second stitch.

Step 2
Knit into the front of the first stitch.

Step 3
Slip both stitches off the left
needle together.

Right twist (t2R)

In this right-sided row twist, the second stitch lies on top and slants to the right,
while the stitch behind is worked through the back of the loop.

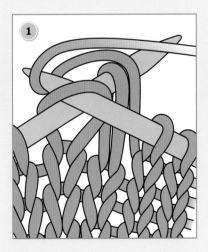 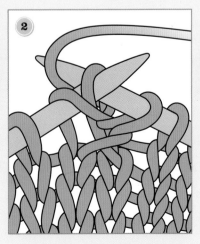 

Step 1
Knit into the front of the second stitch.

Step 2
Knit into the back of the first stitch.

Step 3
Slip both stitches off the left
needle together.

LEARN TO KNIT:
Knitting Essentials

Learning the lingo, understanding needle sizes and being able to change colours are essentials that every keen knitter should know.

Knitting is an enjoyable and rewarding hobby, but sometimes it can be daunting. It may look like a world of meaningless letters and confusing numbers but by learning the lingo and becoming familiar with the tools and techniques, it will all make sense. Knitting abbreviations are one of the trickiest elements of the knitting world, but 'k2tog' does actually mean something. The list opposite will decipher the code and it will soon be second nature. Needles come in a wide variety of sizes. They are your most vital tool so it is important that you know your 6s from your 6mm. Thin needles are required for small and fine projects whereas larger needles are used for chunkier tasks. The chart opposite will help you chose the right needle for your project. We will also guide you through the basics of changing colour for when you are ready to move on.

Changing Colour

Changing colour to create stripes is most easily done at the end of a row. First, knit all the rows that you need to, with your first colour. When you are ready to change colour, drop the old colour. Pick up the new colour by threading the beginning of the new colour through the back of the last stitch and pulling the old colour tightly, trapping the new colour. Hold both the start of the new colour and the end of the old colour together and resume knitting as normal, using the new colour. After every row, pull the end of the new colour to keep it tight, but ensure that the tension is kept even. Cut the old colour, leaving a 15cm/6in tail. Use a tapestry needle to weave the loose ends in.

Needle Conversion Chart

mm	UK	US
2.0mm	14	0
2.25mm	13	1
2.5mm	12	
2.75mm	12	2
3.0mm	11	3
3.25mm	10	3
3.5mm	9	4
3.75mm	9	5
4.0mm	8	6
4.5mm	7	7
5.0mm	6	8
5.5mm	5	9
6.0mm	4	10
6.5mm	3	10½
7.0mm	2	
7.5mm	1	
8.0mm	0	11
9.0mm	00	13
10mm	000	15

Abbreviations

alt	alternate
approx	approximately
beg	beginning
CC	contrast colour
cont	continue
dec	decrease(ing)
DPN	double-pointed needle
foll	following
folls	follows
g st	garter stitch
inc	increase(ing)
k	knit
k2tog	knit 2 together
kfb	knit into front and back of st
KTS	knit the steek st
kwise	knitwise
LH	left hand
m1	make one
m1l	make one left
m1r	make one right
m1p	make one purl
MC	main colour
N1/N2	needle 1/needle 2
p	purl
p2tog	purl 2 together
patt	pattern
pm	place marker
psso	pass slipped st over
pwise	purlwise
rem	remain(ing)
rep	repeat
rnd	round
RH	right hand
RS	right side
sl1	slip 1 st
skpo	sl1, k1, pass sl st over
sm	slip marker
ssk	slip first st, slip second st, then work both together off right-hand needle
st(s)	stitch(es)
st st	stocking stitch
tbl	through back of loop/s
tog	together
w&t	wrap and turn
wyif	with yarn in front
WS	wrong side
yf	yarn forward
yo	yarn over
yon	yarn over needle
yrn	yarn round needle

Accessories

This section contains delightful accessories
to jazz up your outfits, or be given as gifts.
Try out some new techniques and
produce heartfelt, home-made items.

2

INTERMEDIATE

About this
Pattern...

Skills Used
Yarn over or forward
Increasing and decreasing

Yarn Used
Small amounts of DK or aran-weight yarn in pretty colours

Yarn Alternatives
£ *Save:* Acrylic oddments
££ *Spend:* Wool oddments
£££ *Treat:* Cashmere oddments

Tension
28 stitches in 4 inches or 10 cm on needles 3mm (US 2½) if using DK yarn

Notions
Needles to match the yarn you choose, 3.5-4mm for DK and 4.5-5mm for aran

Pattern Notes
Flowers are a great, quick and easy knit – they are small, portable and use tiny amounts of leftover yarn. Experiment and make yourself a whole garden full!

Flower Blossom

Three simple flower patterns that look great when worn as a brooch, attached to a felted bag or mounted on florists wire and placed in a vase.

Flowers are a great way to experiment with new yarns and colours, or dig deep into your oddments collection and use up all of those little pieces of yarn that you've been holding onto for just the right project.

Tension really isn't important when making a flower and with these patterns, it is also not critical that you work the exact amount of rows or increases as specified. Experiment by following the pattern exactly the first time and then adding more or less increase or decrease rows and see how your flower looks.

Whichever flower you make, friends and family will love wearing them!

Cast ON

Flower 1
Cast on 30 stitches.
Beginning with a right-side row, work 6 rows in stocking stitch. Continuing in stocking stitch, increase by knitting twice into every alternate stitch on the next and following 2 right side rows ending with a WS row.
Picot row: K2tog, YO, repeat to end. Purl 1 row before casting off loosely.
Break yarn leaving a tail approx 90cm/36in to assist with sewing up.

Making up
Fold over the picot edge and slip stitch into place on the wrong side to form the pointy top. With wrong side of the flower facing up, place the cast on and cast off tails of yarn down to the cast on row and begin to twist the flower from this corner all the way to the other end. Use the cast on and cast off tails of yarn to twist around the stem of the flower and then sew in place.

Flower 2

Cast on 12 stitches.

Beginning with a knit row,

work 6 rows in stocking stitch.

Next row: Knit twice into each stitch.

Purl 1 row.

Next row: Knit twice into each stitch.

Purl 1 row.

Cast off.

Making up

The cast on edge will be the bottom of your flower. Hold the work the right way up, with the wrong side facing you and roll the flower into shape. You'll need to stitch the bottom to keep it together but there is no need to stitch the edge – it will just look more rose-like if you leave it open.

Experiment with different colours of yarn and buttons when making these flowers

Flower 3

Cast on 48 stitches and beginning with a knit row, work 2 rows in stocking stitch.

Picot row: (Knit 2 together, yarn forward) repeat to end of row.

Continue in stocking stitch for a further 3 rows, ending with a purl row.

First decrease row: Knit 2 together to end of row.

Continue in stocking stitch for a further 3 rows ending with a purl row.

Second decrease row: Knit 2 together to end of row.

Purl next row.

Third decrease row: Knit 2 together to end of row.

Break yarn leaving a tail approx 45cm/18in long. Thread yarn through live stitches on the needle, do not cast off. Draw yarn tight through stitches.

Making up

Sew edges together to form a circle shape. Fold over cast-on edge at picot row to form eyelets and slip stitch the cast-on edge into place. Make a smaller flower the same way by casting on 36 sts and following the same directions or use finer yarn and the same number of sts. Place the smaller circle on top of the larger circle and stitch through centre to hold in place, then add a button in the middle.

Right: These flowers add a feminine touch to any outfit, including the cardigan from page 82!

Pretty in Pink

3

ADVANCED

This gorgeous, delicate knit is perfect for cool summer evenings, and looks sensational in pretty, pastel pink.

About this Pattern...

Skills Used

Decreasing

Lace

Cables

Pick up and knit/purl

Working from a chart

Measurements

Blocked length

2.67m x 59cm/3yd x 23yd

Yarn Used

Adriafil Zephir 50 Classic

Colour 04

1 skein

50% wool, 50% acrylic

100g/1200m/1312yd

cobweb 1 ply

Yarn Alternatives

£ *Save:* ColourMart Cashmere/Wool 1/28 nm

££ *Spend:* Wharfdale Woolworks Baby Alpaca Silk Cobweb Lace

£££ *Treat:* Posh Yarn Miranda Cobweb

Tension

Work 20st and 40 rows in st st to measure 10 x 10cm/4 x 4in using 3mm needles, or size required to obtain tension.

Notions

Circular or long straight needles: 3mm and 4.5mm

Cable needle 2.5mm

Stitch marker

Thread and needle to add lifelines

Pattern starts

Cast ON

Cabled Centre Panel

With 3mm needles cast on:

42 + 2 = 44 sts.

Knit 1 row, turn

Reversed Stocking Stitch

Row 1 (rs): Sl1p, purl to end, turn

Row 2 (ws): Sl1p knit to end, turn

Row 3-6: Repeat row 1 and 2

Pattern Block: Turn at the end of every row

Row 1: Sl1p, p6, k30, p7

Row 2: Sl1k, k6, p30, k7

Row 3: rep row 1

Row 4: rep row 2

Row 5: Sl1p, p6, C6B, five times, p7

Row 6: rep row 2

Row 7 & 9: rep row 1

Row 8 & 10: rep row 2

Row 11: Sl1p, p6, k3 C6F four times, k3, p7

Row 12: Rep row 2

Work rows 1-12 an additional nine times (120 rows in total)

Work row 1-6 once.

Work 6 rows in Reversed st st.

Left side panel

Pick up 75sts along the left side of the cable panel (right side uppermost). Turn. Purl 1 row. Turn.

Special stitch patterns

Sl1p Slip 1 as if to purl

Sl1k Slip 1 as if to knit

C6F (Cable 6 Front) slip the next 3sts onto cable needle, place the cable needle at the front of the work, K next 3sts from left needle, K 3sts from cable needle

C6B (Cable 6 Back) slip the next 3sts onto cable needle, place the cable needle at the back of the work, k next 3sts from left needle, k 3sts from cable needle

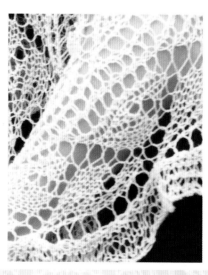

Work pattern chart A

Pattern is worked over 15 sts and should be repeated five times to finish the row.

Work row 1-20 five times (100 rows total)

Row 101-120: work pattern A four times, work pattern chart B once

Row 121-140: work pattern A three times, work pattern B once

Row 141-160: work pattern A two times, work pattern B once

Row 161-180: work pattern A once, work pattern B once

Row 181-199: Work pattern B row 1-19

Row 200: Separately given under pattern chart B

Cast off left panel.

Right side panel

Pick up 75 sts along the right side of the cable panel (right side uppermost). Turn. Purl 1 row. Turn

Work pattern chart A

Pattern is worked over 15 sts and should be repeated five times to finish the row.

Work rows 1-20 five times (100 rows in total)

Row 101-120: work pattern C once, work pattern A four times

Row 121-140: work pattern C once, work pattern A three times

Row 141-160: work pattern C once, work pattern A two times

Row 161-180: work pattern C once, work pattern A once

Row 181-199: work pattern C row 1-19.

Row 200: Separately given under pattern chart C

Cast off right panel.

Border

Starting at the left panel: Pick up stitches around the bottom of the shawl. Turn. (approximately 420 sts)

Row 1: Knit all sts. Turn

Row 2: Sl1k, *yo, k1 (repeat from * to end), turn

Row 3: Sl1k, knit all sts and drop yo

Row 4: repeat row 2

Row 5: repeat row 3

Rows 6 & 7: repeat row 1

Cast off loosely, using: k1, *yo, pass st on right needle over yo, k1, pass stitch over (repeat from *)

Top border

With right side of shawl uppermost – starting on the right-hand side, pick up stitches over the entire length of the shawl. Turn. Work five rows in garter stitch. Cast off. Weave in ends. Block shawl.

Charts

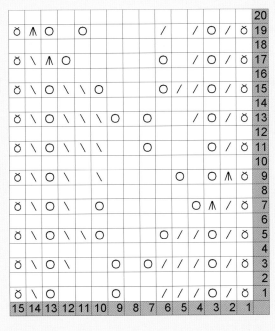

Chart A

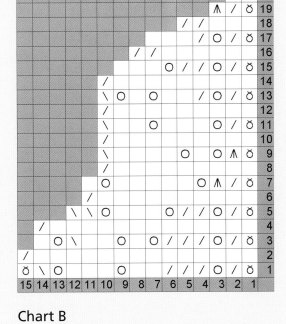

Chart B

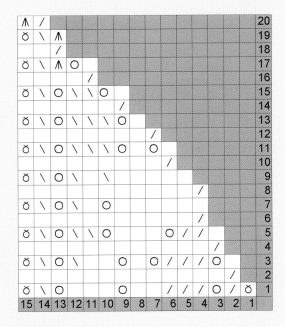

Chart C

Row 200 for chart B

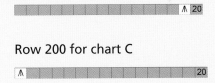

Row 200 for chart C

⋏	double decrease
\	SSK
/	k2tog
ŏ	make back loop
O	yarn over
	knit on right side, purl on wrong side
	no stitch

INTERMEDIATE

Welly Cuffs

Try knitting these charming, leg-warming welly cuffs, to add a splash of style and colour to those crisp, autumn walks.

About this Pattern...

Skills Used

Colourwork
Knitting in the round
Working from a chart
Kitchener stitch
Seaming

Finished Measurements

Stretchy cuff: 32-38cm/12.6-15 in circumference.
Patterned part: 36-38cm/ 14.2-15 in circumference.
Height: before folding: approx 40 cm/ 15.7 in
After folding: approx 20 cm/7.9 in

Yarn Used

Sandness Garn Tove, 100% wool, 50g/160m/175yd, Sport weight – 12 WPI
Colour 4228 (red) 2 balls
Colour 5846 (blue) 1 ball
Gjestal Ullteppegarn, 100% wool, fingering weight – 14 WPI, 50 gr – 200 m – 219 yd
colour 01 (white) 1 ball

Tension

22 sts and 36 rows = 10 x 10cm/ 4 x 4 inches on needles 2.5mm
19 sts and 28 rows = 10 x 10cm/ 4 x 4 inches on needles 3.5mm
(both stockinette stitch)

Notions

Double pointed needles – or circular: 2.5 and 3.5mm – 1 set each
Stitch marker, Tapestry needle

Pattern notes

Chart goes over 28 sts – should be repeated twice to complete the round.

Cast ON

Pattern starts (make two)

Cast on in red and with 2.5mm needles, 84 sts. Divide equally over the needles when working with DPNs, place marker at beginning and after every 28th st when working with circulars.

Cuff

Work 30 rounds in k2, p2 rib

Fold

Purl 1 round
Knit 1 round
Purl 1 round

Part 2 cuff

Work 30 rounds in k2, p2 rib
Knit 1 round
Change to 3.5mm needles.
Join white. Knit 2 rounds in white
Join blue.
Work chart from this point. Chart shows 28 sts and should be repeated twice to complete the round. Chart is worked once in height.
Cut blue.
Knit 2 additional rounds in white. Cut white. Switch to 2.5 mm needles; knit 1 round in red.

Create fold

Purl 1 round
Knit 1 round
Purl 1 round

Yarn Alternatives

£ **Save:** Drops Karisma

££ **Spend:** Jamieson & Smith Jumper Weight

£££ **Treat:** Toft Alpaca DK Yarns

Last part of ribbing

Work 30 rounds in k2, p2 rib. Cast off.
Leave a yarn tail of approx 1m/1yd.
Cut the yarn.

Blocking

The Fair Isle part needs to be blocked lightly.
Pin the patterned part on the blocking
board and leave the ribbed parts as is.
Allow to dry flat.

Finishing

Turn cuff inside-out (wrong side in front of
you). Weave in ends in the Fairisle part of
the cuff. Weave in thread at cast on edge.
Fold the ends towards you – cast on and
cast off edges should 'touch' each other.
Sew top and bottom edge (Kitchener's
stitch), use the strand that was left after
casting off to do so. Weave in remaining
end when done – turn cuff. The right side
will be facing you again.

Wear

The ribbed part will 'disappear' in your
boot. The patterned part stands as a cuff on
top of your boot. Wear and enjoy!

■ One stitch in blue

□ One stitch in white

■ One stitch in red

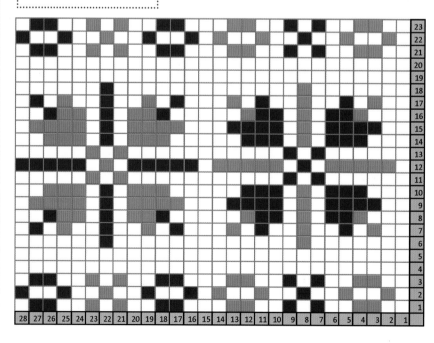

2
INTERMEDIATE

About this Pattern...

Skills Used

Cables
Slipped stitches
Work in the round on DPNs
Increasing and decreasing
Yarn overs
Grafting stitches

Yarn

Schoppel Wolle Zauberball, 75%
superwash wool 25% polyamide,
100g/420m/460yd, WPI 14
Shade 1508 Shadows, 1 ball

Yarn Alternatives

£ **Save:** Drops Delight (2 balls)

££ **Spend:** Trekking Maxima (1 ball)

£££ **Treat:** Crystal Palace Yarns
Mini Mochi (2 balls)

Tension

Work 32 sts and 40 rows to measure
10 x 10cm/4 x 4in in stocking stitch
using smaller needles.

Notions

A set of five 2.25mm (US 1)
double-pointed needles
A set of five 2.5mm (US 1.5)
double-pointed needles
Cable needle
Stitch markers
Tapestry needle

Measurements

To fit foot circumference up to
23cm/9in.

Cable Socks

Woolly socks are a classic project for any knitter.
Comforting and cosy, these cabled socks are
perfect for keeping your toes toasty warm.

Pattern notes

Unless otherwise noted, slip
all sts knitwise with yarn in back.

Cast ON

Pattern starts

With smaller needles, cast on 72 sts,
dividing sts evenly with 18 sts on each
needle.
Join to work in the round, being careful not
to twist sts.
Work in K2, P2 rib for 20 rnds.
Work Rnds 1-8 of Cable and Lace Pattern
seven times, or until leg reaches desired
length, ending with Rnd 8 of patt.

Heel flap

Note: The heel is worked over the first 36
stitches. The Cable and Lace Pattern is
continued on the heel flap. The 36 sts on
last 2 needles are held for the instep.
Row 1 (RS): *K2, p2, sl1, p2, k4, p2, sl1, p2,
k2; rep from * once more. Turn.
Row 2 and all WS rows of Heel Flap: *P2,
k2, p1, k2, p4, k2, p1, k2, p2; rep from *
once more. Turn.
Row 3: *K2tog, yo, p2, sl1, p2, c4f, p2, sl1,
p2, yo, ssk; rep from * once more. Turn.
Row 5: As Row 1.
Row 7: K2tog, yo, p2, sl1, p2, c4b, p2, sl1,
p2, yo, ssk.
Row 8 (WS): As Row 2.
Rep Rows 1-8 until a total of 36 rows have
been completed, ending with Row 4.

Turn heel

Row 1 (RS): K20, k2tog, k1, turn.
Row 2 (WS): Sl1 pwise, p5, p2tog, p1, turn.
Row 3: Sl1 kwise, k6, k2tog, k1, turn.
Row 4: Sl1 pwise, p to 1 st before gap
created in last row, p2tog, p1, turn.
Row 5: Sl1 kwise, knit to 1 st before gap
created in last row, k2tog, k1, turn.
Rep Rows 4-5 until all sts are worked,
ending with a WS row. Turn.

Knit across heel sts. Pick up and knit 18 sts
along side of heel flap, pm, work Row 1 of
Cable and Lace Pattern across held Top of
Foot sts, pm, pick up 18 sts along side of
Heel Flap. K10 and place marker for new
beg of rnd.

If you want matching socks, use two balls of yarn and start both from the same place in the colour sequence.

Gusset

Next rnd: K to m, work Cable and Lace Pattern to m, k to end of rnd.

Next rnd: K to 3 sts before m, yo, sl2, k1, p2sso, work in patt to m, k3tog, yo, k to end of rnd.

Rep last 2 rows until 72 sts remain.

Foot

Next rnd: K to m, work in est patt to m, k to end of rnd.

Rep last Rnd until foot measures 5cm/2in shorter than desired length.

Toe

K 1 rnd.

Dec Rnd: *Knit to 3 sts before marker, k2tog, k1, slip m, k1, ssk; rep from * once more, k to end. (4 sts dec)

Next rnd: Knit.

Rep last 2 rnds seven times more. 40 sts rem

Work Dec Rnd only five times more.

20 sts rem

Finishing

Using Kitchener st, graft toe.

Weave in ends and block, if desired.

Special Stitch Patterns

C4F: Place 2 sts on cable needle in front of work, k2, then k2 from cable needle.

C4B: Place 2 sts on cable needle at back of work, k2, then k2 from cable needle.

Cable and Lace Pattern

Rnd 1: *K2, p2, sl1, p2, k4, p2, sl1, p2, k2; rep from * to end of rnd.

Rnd 2 and all even rnds of leg: *K2, p2, k1, p2, k4, p2, k1, p2, k2; rep from * to end of rnd.

Rnd 3: *K2tog, yo, p2, sl1, p2, c4f, p2, sl1, p2, yo, ssk; rep from * to end of rnd.

Rnd 5: Work as Rnd 1.

Rnd 7: *K2tog, yo, p2, sl1, p2, c4b, p2, sl1, p2, yo, ssk; rep from * to end of rnd.

Rnd 8: Work as Rnd 2.

Rep Rnds 1-8 for pattern.

Cable and Lace Chart

	Knit		5sk		Yo
	Pearl		K2tog		C4B
	Slip				C4F

18 17 16 15 14 13 12 11 10 9 8 7 6 5 4 3 2 1

8 7 6 5 4 3 2 1

Non-matching stripes gives fraternal rather than identical socks.

Noughts & Crosses
Beanie

Snow-surprised Europe and the colours of spring inspired the design of this hat. It uses Fair Isle knitting techniques and comes in two sizes.

Special stitch patterns

Colourwork Pattern (multiple of 10 sts)

Join F.

Rnd 1: K1E, k1F, k6E, k1F, k1E. Rep around.

Rnds 2-3: K2E, k2F, k2E, k2F, k2E. Rep around.

Rnds 4-5: K4E, k2F, k4E. Rep around.

Rnds 6-7: As rnds 2-3.

Rnd 8: As rnd 1.

Rnd 9: K 1 rnd in E.

Join N.

Rnd 10: k2E, k2N, k2E, k2N, k2E. Rep around.

Rnd 11: k1E, k1N, k2E, k2N, k2E, k1N, k1E. Rep around.

Rep rnds 10-11 once more.

Rnd 14: As Rnd 10.

Rnd 15: K 1 round in E.

Join F.

Rnd 16: K1E, k1F, k1E, k4F, k1E, k1F, k1E. Rep around.

Rnd 17: K2E, k1F, k1E, k2F, k1E, k1F, k2E. Rep around.

Rnd 18: K1E, k1F, k1E, k1F, k2E, k1F, k1E, k1F, k1E. Rep around.

Rnds 19-20: k1E, k2F, k1E, k2F, k1E, k2F, k1E. Rep around.

Rnd 21: As rnd 18.

Rnd 22: As rnd 17.

Rnd 23: As rnd 16.

Rnds 24-25: K 2 rnds in E.

Rep pattern rnds 1-25 for pattern.

---

2 INTERMEDIATE

About this Pattern...

Skills Used

Working in the round

Stranded colourwork

Decreasing

Three needle cast off

Measurements

Hat circumference: 50cm/19.5in

(52cm/20.5in)

Yarn Used

Crystal Palace Yarns Mini Solid and Mini Mochi, 80% merino 20% nylon, 50g/178m/195yd, WPI 14

Colour E: Mochi Solid

Colour 1100 Ecru, 1 ball

Colour F: Mini Mochi

Colour 104 Fern Rainbow, 1 ball

Colour N: Mini Mochi

Colour 108 Neptune Rainbow, 1 ball

Yarn Alternatives

£ **Save:** Drops Delight and Drops Merino Extra Fine

££ **Spend:** Schoppel Ombre and Schoppel Zauberball

£££ **Treat:** Malabrigo Sock (variegated and solid)

Notions

A set of five 2.5mm (US 1.5) double-pointed needles

A 2.5mm (US 1.5) circular needle, 40cm/16in long

Stitch markers

Tapestry needle

Tension
Work 32 sts and
42 rows to measure
10 x 10cm or 4 x 4in
in stocking stitch.

Colourwork Chart

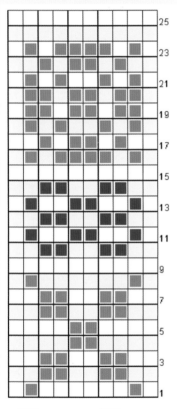

☐ Colour E ▦ Colour F

▧ Colour N

Top Tip

If you're happy using charts, work the colour pattern from the chart (above), or follow the written instructions – both will have the same result!

Cast ON

Brim

Cast on 100 (120) sts in E, if using DPNs dividing them as foll: 30 sts on first needle, 20 (30) sts on second needle, 30 sts on third needle, and 20 (30) sts on last needle. Join for working in the round, being careful not to twist stitches.

Work 20 rnds in k2, p2 rib.
K 1 round.

Colour pattern

Work rnds 1-25 of Colourwork Pattern twice (for a total of 50 rnds of chart/pattern worked).
For the smaller size only: Distribute the sts

so there are 25 sts on each DPN.
Cut all colours but E.

Casting off

Next rnd: With E, k1, ssk, k to 3 sts before end of needle, k2tog, k1. Rep around.
Rep last rnd 9 (12) times more.
20 (16) sts remain.
Turn hat inside out so WS is facing and cast off all sts using three-needle cast off, casting off Needles 1 and 3 together and 2 and 4 together.

Finishing

Weave in ends and block, if desired.

2

INTERMEDIATE

About this
Pattern...

Skills Used

Cables

Knitting in the round

Judy Becker's Magical Cast On

Measurements

7cm/2.7in x 16cm/6.3in and
7cm/2.7in x 17cm/6.7in

Yarns Used

Crystal Palace Yarns - Mini Solid
80% merino, 20% nylon
50g/180m/195yd
4 ply 14 wpi, fingering
Colour 1100 - natural
1 skein

Yarn Alternatives

£ **Save:** Millamia Naturally
Soft merino

££ **Spend:** Drops Delight

£££ **Treat:** Mini Mochi

Tension

Work 28st and 32 rows in st st to
measure 10 x 10cm/4 x 4in using
2.5mm needles, or size required to
obtain tension.

Notions

2.5mm short circular or double
pointed needles
Stitch marker
Cable needle
Needle to weave in ends

Phone•
Cosies

Protect your phone in style with this knitted phone
cosy. With its cool cable knit and button detail,
this little project would make a perfect gift.

Pattern starts

Combine if you like:
Pattern A with cuff C or D
Pattern B with cuff C or D

Cast ON

For both

Cast on two times 18 sts (36sts total).
Knit two rounds.

Pattern A

Rnd 1: *k1, p1, k1, p1, k1, p1, k1, p1, k1*.
Repeat around from * to *.
Rnd 2: knit all sts.
Repeat these two rounds until a height is
reached of 13.5cm/5.3in

Pattern B

Rnd 1 - 4: * p3, k3, p3*, repeat around
from * to *.
Rnd 5: *p2, [Cable: 1 st on cable needle at
the back of your work, k1, p1 from cable
needle], k1, [Cable: 1 st on cable needle in
front of work, p1, k 1 from cable needle],
p2* Repeat around from * to *.
Rnd 6-7: *p2, k1, p1, k1, p1, k1, p2*.
Repeat around from * to *.
Rnd 8: *p1, [Cable: 1 st on cable needle at
the back of your work, k1, p1 from cable
needle], p1, k1,p1, [Cable: 1 st on cable
needle in front of work, p1, k 1 from cable
needle], p1* Repeat around from * to *.

Pattern A

Rnd 9-12: *p1, k1, p2, k1, p2, k1, p1*.
Repeat around from * to *.
Rnd 13: *p1, [Cable: 1 st on cable needle
in front of work, p1, k1 from cable needle],
p1, k1,p1, Cable: 1 st on cable needle at
the back of your work, k1, p1 from cable
needle], p1. Repeat around from * to *.
Rnd 14-15: *p2, k1, p1, k1, p1, k1, p2*.
Repeat around from * to *
Rnd 16: *p2, [Cable: 1 st on cable needle
in front of work, p1, k1 from cable needle],
k1, [Cable: 1 st on cable needle at the back
of your work, k1, p1 from cable needle],
p2*. Repeat around from * to *.
Repeat rnds 1-16 two times, end with
rnd 1-4.

Cuff C

Rnd 1: purl all sts
Rnd 2: knit all sts.
Repeat rnds 1 & 2 to work 20 rnds in total

Cuff D

Work 20 rounds in k2 p2 rib.
Cast off sts loosely. Weave in ends.

Pattern B

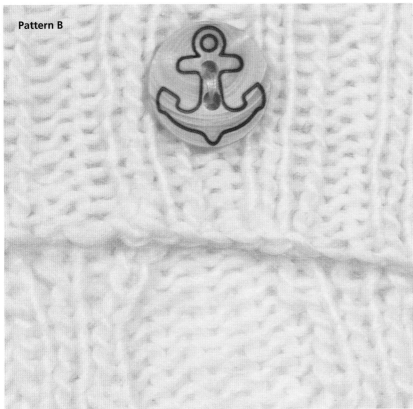

Top Tip

Make sure your stitches are loose when knitting with this yarn

1
BEGINNER

Handspun Snug

Combining an open-lace pattern with a super-chunky handspun yarn produces a warm, yet lightwight, giant winter scarf.

About this
Pattern...

Skills Used
Yarns over

Finished Measurements
179 x 19cm/70.5 x 7.5in

Yarn Used
Camilla's Handspun Yarn Merino, Wool 700g/78m/85yd WPl 3
Colour: Hello Sailor - 1 Ball

Yarn Alternatives
£ **Save:** Wendy Serenity Super Chunky

££ **Spend:** Twilley Freedom Wool Super Chunky

£££ **Treat:** Colinette Point 5

Tension
4 stitches x 3 rows = 10 x 10cm/4 x 4in using 20mm needles.

Notions
20mm needles

Special stitch patterns
Mesh stitch pattern.
Row 1: KNIT
Row 2: K1, **YO, K2tog**
Repeat work in ** to last stitch K1

Pattern notes
Make sure your stitches are as loose as possible when knitting with this yarn – if your tension is too tight, your scarf will be stiff and uncomfortable to wear. Pull the stitches loose or use 2 x 20mm needles at once if you can't get a loose enough tension.

Snug
Cast on 8 stitches.
Work in Mesh stitch pattern until you have 1m/1yd of yarn left, ending with row 1.
Cast off.

Finishing
Darn in the cast on and cast off end.
Pull the stitches into shape.

Cast ON

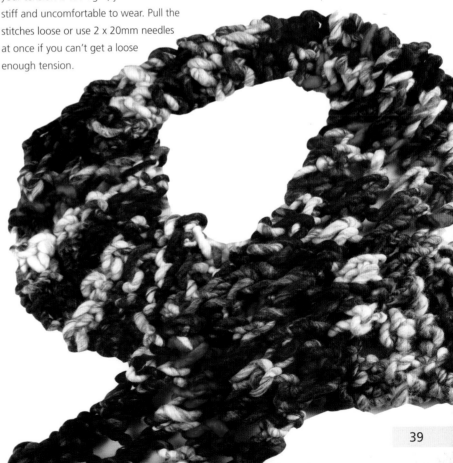

Little Green Bag

This adorable bag is the perfect project for those looking to improve their skills. With a detailed knit, this cute bag oozes style.

Special stitch patterns

Pattern A

Rnd 1: *k3, yf twice, k3 *repeat

Rnd 2: *k3, drop yfs to create long st Working next 3 sts together (k1, p1, k1) in front loops. *repeat

Rnd 3: *yf twice, k6 *repeat

Rnd 4: *Drop yfs to create long st working next 3 sts together (k1, p1, k1) in front loops, k3. *repeat

Repeat rounds 1-4

Pattern B

Rnd 1: sl1 knitwise, p1, k8, p1, sl1 knitwise

Rnd 2: k1, p1, k8, p1, k1

Rnd 3: Rep rnd 1

Rnd 4: Rep rnd 2

Rnd 5: Sl1 knitwise, p1, move 2sts to cable needle at front of work, k2, k2 sts from cable needle, move 2sts to cable needle at the back of work, k2, k2sts from cable needle, p1, slip 1 knitwise

Rnd 6: Rep rnd 2

Rnd 7: Rep rnd 1

Rnd 8: k1, p1, k2, move 2sts to back of work, k2, k2sts from cable needle, k2, p1, k1

Repeat rows 1-8

About this Pattern...

Skills Used

Increasing
Decreasing
Cables
Lace
Knitting in the round
Basic Crochet

Measurements

Small: 19 x 35cm/7.4 x 13.7in
Large: 25 x 35cm/9.8 x13.7in

Yarns Used

John Arbon (Fibre Harvest LTD)
Knit by Numbers
Content of yarn e.g. 100% merino,
DK 100g, 250m, 273yds
WPI 11
Colour: KBN 56
1 skein

Yarn Alternatives

£ **Save:** Drops Lima

££ **Spend:** Cascade Ultra Pima

£££ **Treat:** Debbie Bliss Rialto DK

Tension

Work 22st and 29 rows in Stockinette st to measure 10 x 10cm /4 x 4in using 4mm needles, or size required to obtain tension.

Notions

2 x 4mm circular needles
4mm crochet hook
4mm cable needle
Tapestry needle

Cast ON

Pattern starts

Use hook to make a chain of 36(48) sts.
With circ 1: pick up and knit through front
loops of the chain until you have 36(48)
sts on the needle. With second circ, pick
up and knit 36(48) loops. Knit 1 rnd– mark
beginning and half-way point

Divide for front and back

Front: Work 12(18)sts in pattern A, 12sts in
B, 12(18)sts in A
Back: Work 12(18)sts in pattern A, 12sts in
B, 12(18)sts in A
Continue in pattern for 56 rounds, or until
height desired

Handles

Rnd 1: knit all sts
Rnd 2: purl all sts
Repeat rounds 1-2 until a total of 10 rounds
have been worked
Rnd 11: k9(15), cast off 18sts, k9(15),
k9(15), cast off 18, k9(15)
Rnd 12: p9(15), cast on 18sts, p9(15),
p9(15), cast on 18sts, p9(15)
Rnd 13-24: Repeat steps 1-2. Cast off all
sts. Weave in ends

2
INTERMEDIATE

About this Pattern...

Skills used

Increasing and decreasing

Cables

Pick up and knit

Knitting in the round

Working from a chart

Beading

Measurements

Height: 21cm/18.2in

Circumference 19.5cm /7.5in

(measured above thumb) for the

model size

(sizes given: 19-20cm/7.5-8in and

21.5cm/8.5in circumference)

Yarn Used

Gjestal Ullteppegarn – 100% wool

Colour: 12 - blue

1 ball – 50 grams – 200m. Fingering

weight, 14 wpi

Notions

1 set Double Pointed Needles 2.5 mm

(or circular needle in same size)

Stitch marker

Safety pin

Darning needle to weave in ends

Approximately 600 beads.

(Rocailles with a 0.8 mm opening)

Crochet hook 0.75 mm

Tension

Work 28 st and 32 rows in Stockinette

st to measure 10 x 10cm/4 x 4in using

2.5 mm needles, or size required to

obtain tension.

Butterfly
Fingerless Gloves

Be unique with these dainty butterfly gloves.
With adorable detail and a cosy knit, these will
keep you warm and stylish throughout the year.

Special stitch patterns

Chart stitch in brown: Place bead on a
0.75 mm hook, hook needle onto the
stitch, transfer bead into your work, put
stitch to the left needle; Knit stitch.
Chart stitch in blue: Knit stitch.
BL: Make 1 Back Loop

Pattern starts

Cast on 48 (52-56) sts.
Join carefully. Circular knitters:
mark beginning and halfway point.
Cuff: Work in k2 p2 rib for 20 rounds.
Continue: Knit 20 rounds.

Cast ON

Divide work

The first 24 (26-28) sts are for the top of
the hand. You will start with row1 from the
chart; according to your size. (S: 24 sts – M:
26 sts – L: 28 sts)

How to work

The sts for the bottom of the hand: Mark
for thumb gusset.

Left glove

Thumb gusset will be worked over the last
12-14-16 sts. The first 12 sts for every size
will be knit.

Yarn Alternatives

£ *Save:* Jamieson and Smith 2 ply
Jumper weight (2 x 25 gr needed)

££ *Spend:* Drops Alpaca

£££ *Treat:* The Knitting Goddess Yarns;
4 ply Merino & Bamboo

43

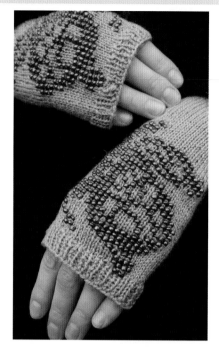

Charts

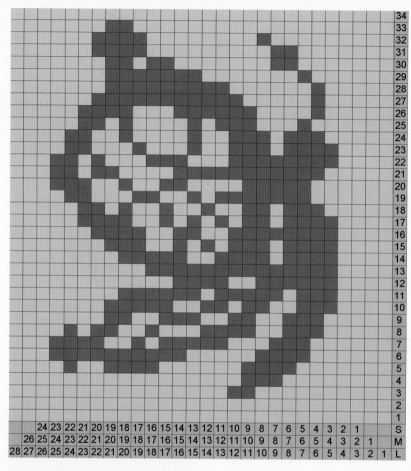

Above: Chart B (option for left mitten)

Right: Chart A

Right glove

Thumb gusset will be worked over the first 12-14-16 sts. The last 12 sts for every size will be knit.

Thumb gusset

1: k2 (3-4), BL, k8, BL, k2 (3-4)

2: knit sts

3: k2 (3-4), BL, k10, BL, k2 (3-4)

4: knit sts

5: k2 (3-4), BL, k12, BL, k2 (3-4)

6: knit sts

7: k2 (3-4), BL, k14, BL, k2 (3-4)

8: knit sts

9: k2 (3-4), BL, k16, BL, k2 (3-4)

10: knit sts

11: k2 (3-4), BL, k18, BL, k2 (3-4)

12: knit sts

13: k2 (3-4), BL, k20 BL, k2 (3-4)

14: knit sts

15: k2 (3-4), BL, k22, BL, k2 (3-4)

16: knit sts

17: k2 (3-4), BL, k24, BL, k2 (3-4)

18: k7 (8-9) set aside 16 on safety pin, BL2, k7 (8-9)

19: k6 (7-8), SSK, K2tog, k6(7-8)

20-34: Knit all sts. Knit 1 additional round. Continue with 5 rounds in k1, p1 rib. Cast off sts.

Thumb: Place sts on the needles, from the safety pin. Pick up an additional 8 sts around thumb gap. Work 5 round in k1 p1 rib. Cast off stitches. Weave in all ends. Work second fingerless glove. Block gloves.

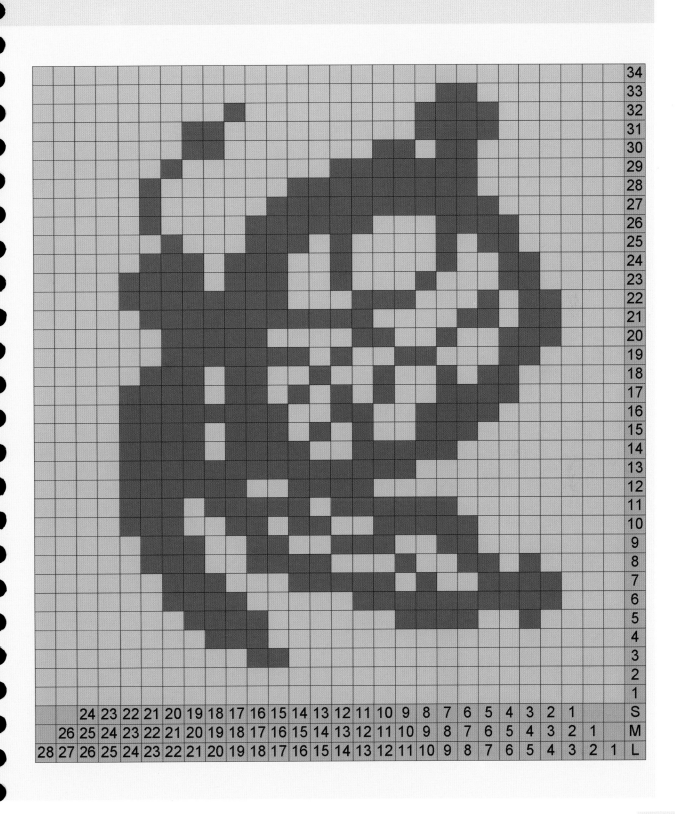

2

INTERMEDIATE

About this
Pattern...

Measurements
One size to fit average woman's foot

Yarn Used
Crystal Palace Panda Cotton (55% bamboo, 24% cotton, 21% elastic nylon, 50g/157m/170yd), 2 balls shade 406 Caribbean Blue (MC), WPI 14
Crystal Palace Panda Superwash (51% bamboo, 39% superwash wool, 10% nylon, 50g/168m/186yd), 1 ball shade 2009 Joyful (CC), WPI 14

Yarn Alternatives
£ **Save:** Lang, Opal
££ **Spend:** Noro, Kureyon Sock
£££ **Treat:** Skein Queen, Elegance

Notions
2mm (US 0) circular or double-pointed needles
2.5mm (US 1) circular or double-pointed needles
Tapestry needle
Stitch markers

Tension
Work 32 sts and 44 rows to measure 4in/10cm in stocking st with larger needles

Top Tip
Using multicoloured yarn in a patterned piece like this adds that extra little something without a lot of work!

Joyful Socks

These charming rose-print socks will bring joy to anyone's heart!

Stitch instructions
2x2 Rib
Multiple of 4 sts
Rnd 1: *K2, p2; rep from * to end.
Rep Rnd 1.

3-Needle cast off
Have stitches to be joined on two separate needles, held parallel with right sides facing. Insert third (working) needle into first st on front needle, then first st on back needle and k these sts together as if they were one. *Insert third needle into next st on front needle, then next st on back needle and k together as if they were one. Slip first stitch over second st and off needle to cast off 1 stitch. Rep from * until required number of sts have been cast off.

Leg
With smaller needles and MC, cast on 64 sts. Join being careful not to twist, place markers every 16 sts (4 markers) if working on circulars, otherwise divide sts evenly over 4 DPN. Work 2x2 Rib for 20 rnds.
Change to larger needles and k 5 rnds.
Join CC, work Rnds 1-17 of chart. Chart is 32 sts wide and should be worked twice, once each side of the sock. Cut CC.
K 5 rnds.

Cast ON

Heel flap
Place 32 sts on holder for instep.
Working on rem sts only:
Row 1 (RS): *Sl1, k1; rep from * to end.
Row 2 (WS): Sl1, purl to end.
Rep Rows 1-2 for a total of 32 rows.
RS is facing for next row.

Chart

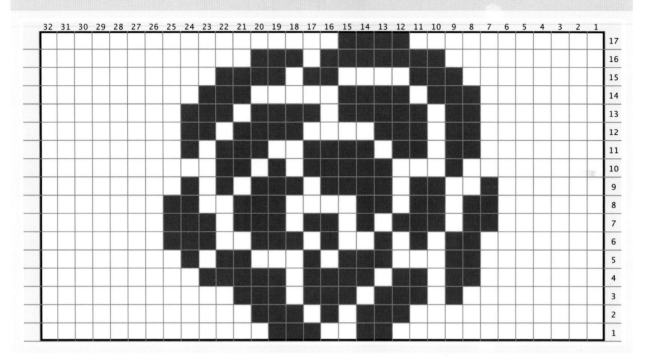

Turn heel

Row 1: K18, k2tog, k1, turn.
Row 2: Sl1, p5, p2tog, p1, turn.
Row 3: Sl1, k to 1 st before gap, k2tog, k1, turn.
Row 4: Sl1, p to 1 st before gap, p2tog, p1, turn.
Rep Rows 3-4 until all heel sts have been worked. 22 sts rem. RS is facing for next row.

Gusset

Join CC and work (k1 MC, k1 CC) across heel sts, pm. Pick up and knit 16 sts along side of heel flap, alternating 1 st MC, 1 st CC, pm. Work 32 instep sts following chart, pm. Pick up and knit 16 sts along side of heel flap, alternating colours as before, pm. 86 sts.
Rnd 1: Work in established patt (k1 MC, k1 CC) over sole and gusset sts and chart over instep sts.
Rnd 2: Work in patt over heel sts, sl marker, k2tog, k to end of gusset. Work chart patt

over instep sts. Work to last 2 gusset sts, ssk. Rep Rnds 1-2 until 64 sts rem.
AT THE SAME TIME, when Row 17 of chart is complete, work 5 rnds in MC only over instep sts.

Foot

Continue working sole sts in stripe pattern. Work chart again over instep sts. When second rep of chart is complete, cut CC and work 5 rnds stocking st with MC over all sts.

Toe

Rnd starts at beg of sole sts.
Rnd 1: K1, ssk, k to last 3 sole sts, k2tog, k1, k1, ssk, k to last 3 instep sts, k2tog, k1.
Rnd 2: Knit.
Rep Rnds 1-2 until 40 sts rem, then Rnd 1 only until 20 sts rem.

Turn sock inside out. Use 3-Needle Cast Off to close toe. Weave in ends.

INTERMEDIATE

About this
Pattern...

Measurements
At widest point after blocking:
124cm/49in

Yarn Used
3 skeins Louet Mooi (50g/320m/350yd,
70% bamboo, 15% bison,
15% cashmere), shade 03 Amethyst
Wraps per inch (WPI): 16

Yarn Alternatives
£ *Save:* Knitting Goddess,
  3 ply cashmere

££ *Spend:* Malabrigo, Laceweight

£££ *Treat:* Knitwitches, Lace Silk

Notions
4mm (US 6) double-pointed needles
4mm (US 6) circular needle,
60cm/24in long
Stitch markers
Tapestry needle

Pattern Notes
Knitted in the round from the
centre outward.

Special Instructions
The trickiest part of this shawl is
the first few rounds on DPNs. Once
you have the pattern established it
becomes easier to see the stitches
and when you have enough on
your needles you can swap to a
longer circular needle.

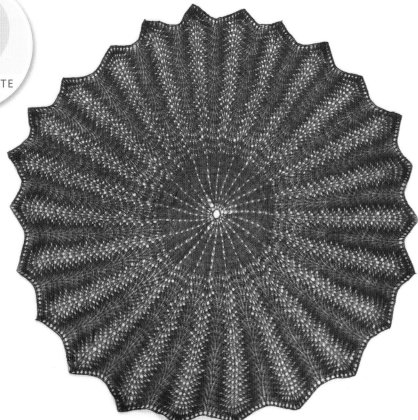

Shawl

This circular shawl is knitted
from the centre out in a
luxury laceweight yarn.

Cast
ON

Centre of shawl
With double-pointed needles, cast on 12 sts.
Pm and join for working in the round.
Rnd 1: Knit.
Rnd 2: *Yo, k1; rep from * to end. 24 sts.
Rnds 3-4: Rep Rnds 1-2. 48 sts.
Rnds 5-7: Knit.
Rnd 8: *Yo, k2; rep from * to end. 72 sts.
Rnds 9-11: Knit.

Rnd 12: *Yo, k3; rep from * to end. 96 sts.
Change to circular needle when necessary.
Rnds 13-15: Knit.
Rnd 16: *Yo, k4; rep from * to end. 120 sts.
Continue to increase 24 sts on every 4th
rnd as set, working 1 more st between yos
on each inc rnd, to 240 sts (Rnd 36).
K 3 rnds.

Begin feather and fan

Rnd 40: *(Yo, k1) twice, k2tog three times, (yo, k1) twice; rep from * to end. 264 sts.

Rnds 41-43 and all rnds not otherwise specified: Knit.

Rnd 44: *(Yo, k1) twice, k2tog three times, k1, (yo, k1) twice; rep from * to end. 288 sts.

Rnd 48: *(Yo, k1) twice, yo, k2tog four times, (yo, k1) twice; rep from * to end. 312 sts.

Rnd 52: *(Yo, k1) three times, k2tog four times, (yo, k1) twice; rep from * to end. 336 sts.

Rnd 56: *(Yo, k1) three times, k2tog four times, k1, (yo, k1) twice; rep from * to end. 360 sts.

Rnd 60: *(Yo, k1) twice, yo, k2tog five times, (yo, k1) three times; rep from * to end. 384 sts.

Rnd 64: *(Yo, k1) three times, k2tog five times, (yo, k1) three times; rep from * to end. 408 sts.

Rnd 68: *(Yo, k1) three times, k2tog five times, k1, (yo, k1) three times; rep from * to end. 432 sts.

Rnd 72: *(Yo, k1) three times, yo, k2tog six times, (yo, k1) three times; rep from * to end. 456 sts.

Rnd 76: *(Yo, k1) four times, k2tog six times, (yo, k1) three times; rep from * to end. 480 sts.

Rnd 80: *(Yo, k1) four times, k2tog six times, k1, (yo, k1) three times; rep from * to end. 504 sts.

Rnd 84: *(Yo, k1) three times, yo, k2tog seven times, (yo, k1) four times; rep from * to end. 528 sts.

Rnd 88: *(Yo, k1) four times, k2tog seven times, (yo, k1) four times; rep from * to end. 552 sts.

Rnd 92: *(Yo, k1) four times, k2tog seven times, k1, (yo, k1) four times; rep from * to end. 576 sts.

Rnd 96: *(Yo, k1) four times, yo, k2tog eight times, (yo, k1) four times; rep from * to end. 600 sts.

Rnd 100: *(Yo, k1) five times, k2tog eight times, (yo, k1) four times; rep from * to end. 624 sts.

Rnd 104: *(Yo, k1) five times, k2tog eight times, k1, (yo, k1) four times; rep from * to end. 648 sts.

Rnd 108: *(Yo, k1) four times, yo, k2tog nine times, (yo, k1) five times; rep from * to end. 672 sts.

Rnd 112: *(Yo, k1) five times, k2tog nine times, (yo, k1) five times; rep from * to end. 696 sts.

Rnd 116: *(Yo, k1) five times, k2tog nine times, k1, (yo, k1) five times; rep from * to end. 720 sts.

Rnd 120: *(Yo, k1) five times, yo, k2tog ten times, (yo, k1) five times; rep from * to end. 744 sts.

Rnd 124: *(Yo, k1) six times, k2tog ten times, (yo, k1) five times; rep from * to end. 768 sts.

Rnd 128: *(Yo, k1) six times, k2tog ten times, k1, (yo, k1) five times; rep from * to end. 792 sts.

Rnd 132: *(Yo, k1) five times, yo, k2tog eleven times, (yo, k1) six times; rep from * to end. 816 sts.

Rnd 136: *(Yo, k1) six times, yo, k2tog eleven times, (yo, k1) six times; rep from * to end. 840 sts.

Rnd 140: *(Yo, k1) six times, k2tog eleven times, k1, (yo, k1) six times; rep from * to end. 864 sts.

Rnd 141: Knit.

Rnd 142: Purl.

Rnd 143: *Yo, k2tog; rep from * to end.

Rnd 144: Knit.

Rnd 145: Purl.

Cast off loosely. Weave in ends, and block. and wet block firmly.

Stylish Wristwarmers

Wristwarmers are a good way to practise new designs, as they use up small amounts of yarn and are quick and fun to knit.

2
INTERMEDIATE

Pattern notes

The chart that you choose to use should be in the region of 18 rows high and either 44 stitches wide or a number that can be divided by 44. If you wanted to use a chart that was 10 stitches wide you could either add in some plain stitches either side or decrease the number of stitches to 40.

If you want to turn this design into fingerless gloves you would simply knit them longer and either knit them flat and seam together leaving a space for your thumb or you could cast off a large buttonhole for your thumb to go through if you want to knit them in the round. Or why not use this as a good opportunity to try a steek?

Pattern starts

Cast on 44 stitches using solid yarn and join to work in round. Work in 2 x 2 rib for 15 rounds. Continue in stocking stitch for 2 rounds. Switch to a 2 round solid and 2 round multicoloured yarn stripe pattern and work 18 rounds in stocking stitch in total. Continue in multicoloured yarn and work 1 round of eyelets as below: (K2tog YO) Repeat to last 2 stitches, K2tog Work 2 more rounds in stocking stitch. Cast off.

Cast ON

Finishing

Fold over and sew the picot/eyelet row in place so that the picots are on top of the hand.

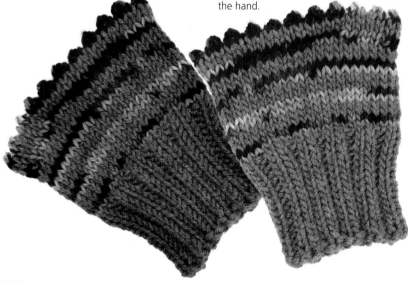

About this Pattern...

Skills Used
Knitting in the round
YOs

Finished Measurements
15 x 12cm / 5.9 x 4.7in

Yarns Used
Colinette Cadenza DK - Bright Charcoal Rowan Wool DK - Grey Oddments of each

Yarn Alternatives
- (£) *Save:* Wendy Bliss Merini
- (££) *Spend:* Debbie Bliss Rialto DK
- (£££) *Treat:* Fibre Company - Acadia

Tension
18 stitches and 24 rows to 10cm over stocking stitch using 4.5mm needles

Notions
4.5mm DPNs or circulars
Darning needle

Top Tip

Wristwarmers are the perfect canvas for experimenting as they are small and quick to knit.

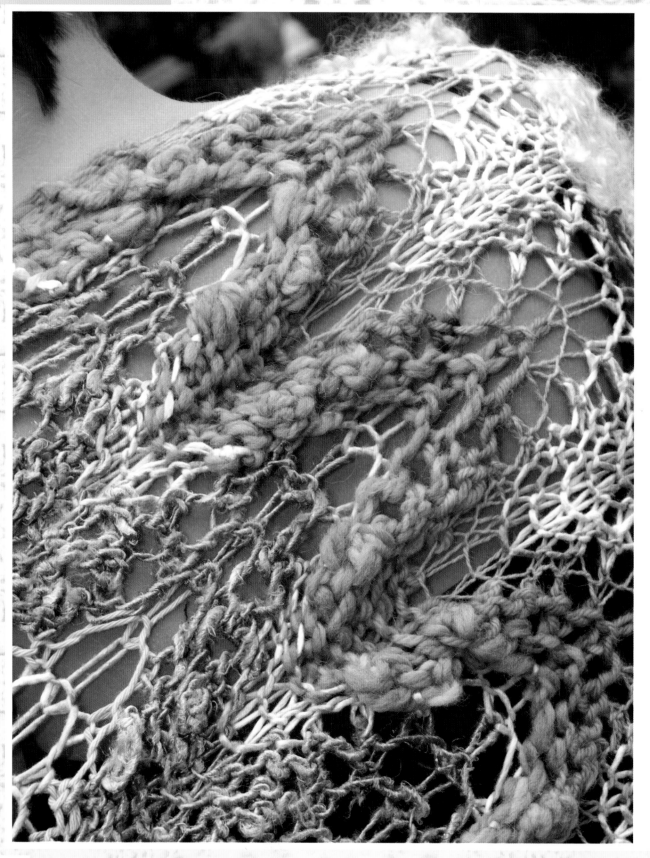

2

INTERMEDIATE

About this
Pattern...

Measurements

Stole shown: about 50 x 200cm/
20 x 80in

Yarn Used

Approx. 18 oz. [500g] of odds and
ends for the stole

Needles

Straight or circular needle of size
appropriate for your yarn. We used US
15 (10mm) for the stole

Thrifty
Shawl

Use up all your loose odds and ends to make this
unique and cosy shawl.

To avoid lots of joins it is recommended that where a new yarn is being joined in, that it is woven in with the old yarn. To do this leave 20cm/8in of the old yarn, twist around the new yarn before knitting in, making sure that ends are concealed. If joining new yarn at the start of a new row, alternate joins between the knit rows and purl rows. For the stole (left) we used approx 500g of odds and ends of HipKnits yarns. You could use one colour of hand-painted variegated yarn throughout, the effect would be less colourful but would still show off the yarns beautifully.

Scallop Pattern

Multiple of 18 sts
Row 1 (RS): *(K2tog) 3 times,
(YO, k1) 6 times, (k2tog) 3 times;
rep from * to end.
Row 2 (WS): Purl.

Pattern starts

Cast on 60 sts.
Knit 3 rows.
Next row (RS): K3, work Row 1 of Scallop
Pattern over next 54 sts, k3.

Cast ON

Next row (WS): K3, purl to last 3 sts, k3.
Continue in pattern as set, keeping 3
sts at each side in garter stitch, until
wrap is desired length, ending with
a WS row.
Knit 3 rows.
Bind off.

Finishing

Weave in any ends. Press lightly with
a damp cloth.

Tunia Scarf

This lovely piece will take you from summer through to autumn.

This beautiful pattern is simple to knit and shows off variegated yarns beautifully. The stitch pattern creates a natural bias shape to the fabric and just 1 skein of sock yarn makes a super long scarf that can be wrapped around your neck or left to hang down. You could use any hand-painted yarn for this project, just make sure that the needle size is appropriate to the weight of the yarn.

Bias Eyelet Pattern
Multiple of 2 sts

Row 1 (WS): **Purl.**
Row 2 (RS): **K1, *YO, k2tog; rep from *** to last st, **k1.**
Rep Rows 1-2 for pattern.

Pattern
Cast on 30 sts. Work in Bias Eyelet Pattern for 118" [300 cm], or to desired length, ending with a WS row.
Bind off.

Finishing
Weave in ends. Block.

About this Pattern...

Finished Measurements
Approx 15 x 300cm/6 x 118in

Yarn
1 skein HipKnits sock yarn

Tension
Work 22 sts and 30 rows to measure 4 x 4in, 10 x 10cm Bias Eyelet Pattern

Notions
US 7 [4.5 mm] straight needles
Tapestry needle

Lovely Legwarmers

Legwarmers are a simple project to make and once you have the basic pattern in your head you can add colourwork, cables or lace patterns.

Pattern starts

Cast on 72 stitches and join for working in the round.

Work 12 rows in 1 x 1 rib.

Change to 2 x 2 rib and work in this stitch for approx 15cm/6in.

Change to 3 x 3 rib and work in this stitch for approx 10cm/4in.

Change back to 2 x 2 rib for approx 15cm/6in.

Change back to 1 x 2 rb for 10 rows. Make a second legwarmer in the same way. Sew in ends and wear.

Cast
ON

About this Pattern...

Skills Used

Knitting in the round

Cast on and off

Yarn Used

100g 4 ply yarn, we like Artesano Alpaca which comes in a great range of colour.

Tension

28 stitches and 32 rows to 10cm over stocking stitch using 3mm needles

Notions

3mm DPNs or circulars

Darning needle

Tapestry needle

1

BEGINNER

About this
Pattern...

Skills Used

Increasing

Decreasing

Pick up and knit

Working from a chart

Basic crochet

Measurements

Length: 85cm/33.5in

Width: 160cm/63in

Yarns Used

Artesano Superfine Alpaca DK

100% Alpaca

50g/100m/109 yards

x4 3138 Uruguay

x4 SNF10 Cream

0178 Peru for red trim and charted swatches

5340 Brazil for green in charted swatches

Yarn Alternatives

£ *Save:* King Cole Baby Alpaca DK

££ *Spend:* Rowan Baby Alpaca DK

£££ *Treat:* Knit Shop 'Fino' Alpaca

Tension

Work 22 st and 30 rows in garter st to measure 10 x 10cm/4 x 4in using 4mm needles, or size required to obtain tension.

Notions

4mm Needles (long)

Stripey Shawl

This shawl will take the chill off Spring-evening beach walking and has a wonderful nautical feel.

Pattern starts

This is a simple project that's ideal for the beginner knitter and gives a really beautiful and versatile shawl that can be worn in a variety of ways.

Cast ON

Work in garter stitch (knit every row) throughout working 2 rows in MC and 2 rows in CC. Do not cut the yarn in-between the striped rows, just carry it up the side.

A chunky knit with a distinctively modern twist, you'll be the star of the show in this beautiful shawl.

Increase 1 stitch at the beginning of every other row so that you end up with one straight edge, and one sloping edge.
Repeat this until your work measures approx 84cm/33 in from the cast on edge.
From now on you will be decreasing instead of increasing so that the slope goes back the other way.
Continue until you have 3 stitches left.
Cast off.
Using a contrasting colour, make 3 tassles and sew one to each point of the triangle.

Tassels

To make the tassels, wind some wool several times around two needles that are spaced evenly apart from each other. While taught, tie a length of the wool around the middle of the strands.
Tie this off and slide off the needles.
Cut the ends of the wool so they're all separate strands and fold the strands over so they're hanging.
Tie another length of yarn around the strands, approximately 2cm/1in from the fold, fasten tightly and enjoy!

Added extras

For a little something extra, why not add a crochet trim to the border edge?

Option 1

Round 1 - Using red yarn, pick up and knit 1 stitch in every stitch along the 3 sides of the shawl. Ensure that the yarn is not pulled too tightly otherwise the edging will bunch in.
Round 2 - Cast off all stitches.

Option 2

Crochet picot edging
Insert hook into first st. Ch 3. Dc into first ch and Dc in next st. Rep to end.

Charts

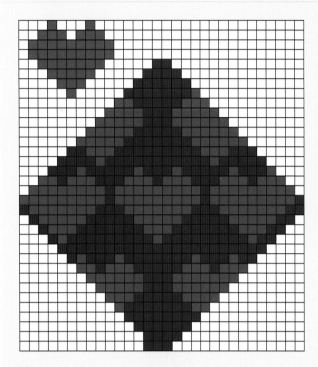

Hearts

Example of a knitted anchor

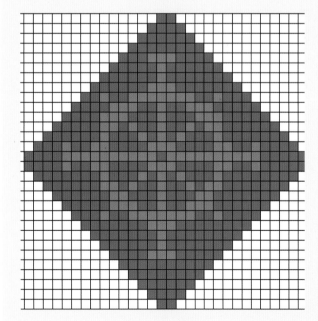

Wheel

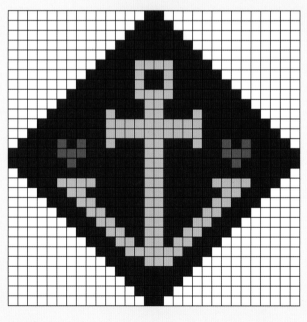

Anchor

Charts

These charts have been designed to fit neatly into the
bottom of the shawl's triangle. Using stranded colourwork
technique, you can add a splash of colour to your shawl.

Cast on 2 stitches and using K1f&b (Knit 1 front and
back) add 2 stitches either end, to every other row.

In st st, knit until you have 28 stitches.

If you'd like to add button holes, increase the next row at
either end with YO.

Knit to 30 stitches and then start decreasing, using SSK
and K2TOG until you have 2 stitches left on your needle.

Cast off.

Flower Headband

Young, fashionable, simple to knit and fun to wear,
this funky flower headband will help you banish
even the worst bad hair day!

About this Pattern...

Pattern starts

For the main part of the
headband cast on 10 stitches
in MC and work in 2 x 2 rib until the
length of the work measures 50cm/20in
or the right length to comfortably wrap
around your head.

Cast off and sew together with right sides
facing to make a snugly fitting headband.

Flower

Cast on 10 stitches in CC and work 5 rows in
stocking stitch.

Increase in every other stitch on the next and
following 3 right side rows.
Next (Picot) row
K1, YO, K2tog repeat to end.
Work 2 more rows in stocking stitch and then
cast off.

Finishing

Fold the picot edge of the flower over and
stitch in place. Roll the flower with the
wrong side facing up until it spirals into a
flower shape. Sew in place and
attach to headband.

Skills Used

Decreasing
Knitting in the round
Knitting in rows

Finished Measurements

8cm/3.1in long by 4cm/1.6 in wide

Yarn Used

Debbie Bliss Cashmerino aran, scraps
of two different colours

Tension

Work 45 st and 20 rows in stocking
st to measure 10 x 10cm/4 x 4in
using 2.0mm needles, or size required
to obtain tension. Note that these
are much smaller needles than
recommended for this yarn.

Notions

4mm needles
Darning needle

Womenswear

Dive into more complex projects in this exciting clothing section, and knit your very own vibrant, one-of-a-kind garments that you will want to wear time and time again.

BASIC GARMENT
Alterations

If you're wearing a sweater made just for you, shouldn't it fit perfectly? This simple guide gives you the basics to adapt any pattern to suit your shape.

Knowing your own body shape is critical for knitting garments that fit you perfectly. Not every pattern that you fall in love with is going to look as good on you as it does in the magazine, so here is a brief introduction to understanding what you need to change in order to get a perfect custom fit.

Finding your ideal measurements

Find a favourite sweater or cardigan (hand-knitted or shop-bought) and lay it out on a flat surface. Grab a pencil, paper and tape measure and get ready to measure.

The key measurements to take are: length of sleeve from armpit to cuff; length from armpit to bottom of garment; length from armpit to shoulder; bust; and bottom edge of garment. Using our

blank schematic (below right), record the exact measurements of these points on your favourite garment and then compare them with the measurements given on the schematic of the garment you wish to make.

Some differences are much easier to amend than others. You also need to remember that the stitch pattern that the garment is knitted in will have an impact on how complicated it will be to alter the pattern to fit you perfectly.

Don't skip the swatch!

Before you start working out how to alter the pattern, you need to knit a tension square. This is a step that even many experienced knitters will ignore, but any designer or pattern alterer will tell you it is a critical step in ensuring that you are knitting to the exact size that the pattern is written for, as well as in understanding the drape and texture of the yarn that you are using.

Look at the pattern. If a lace or cable stitch is involved, it is best to make two swatches. If it is knitted in stocking stitch, cast on half a dozen stitches more than the pattern recommends for 10cm/4in and work until you have a square.

Measure your swatch and using our blank swatch picture (left), write down the tension

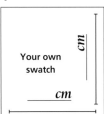

Your own swatch

cm

cm

Altering sleeve length

Sleeves that are longer or shorter than your ideal garment are probably among the easiest amendments to make. By looking at your sleeve measurement on the blank schematic, you will easily be able to see how many inches or centimetres you need to add or reduce to make it fit. Compare this with your tension square to see how those inches convert to rows, and that is how many extra or fewer rows you will need to knit. The best place to alter on a sleeve is just after the cuff stitches, before any shaping takes place. For instance, if the sleeve starts with 10 rows of 2x2 rib, don't attempt to add or remove any rows until you have completed this.

Lengthen sleeve above cuff.

Your own schematic.

of your swatch (the number of stitches and rows per 10cm/4in square) and then check this against the tension of the pattern that you want to knit.

Altering body length

Looking at it from a very simplistic point of view, is the garment you want to make longer or shorter in the body than the one you have chosen as your ideal fit? This will tell you whether you need to increase or decrease rows from the body of the pattern, using your tension swatch as before.

Does the pattern you want to make have waist shaping? If so, you will need to ensure that this shaping remains in place. If your perfect-fit sweater includes waist shaping, measure how far from the bottom this shaping takes place and make sure that when you add or remove rows, you don't move the waist shaping. By carefully reading the pattern you wish to make, you will be able to see where the waist shaping will fall in comparison to your ideal. Most alterations to body length are best done just above the hem.

Altering the hem width

The number of stitches that you cast on (assuming that you are knitting a bottom-up garment) will determine the width of the bottom of the piece. If the garment is to end around your hips, you might need to customise this for a personal fit. Adding or removing stitches at the cast-on edge will make the bottom of your garment either wider or narrower. Bear in mind that you'll need to make the back and front the same, and that if the garment features an allround

lace pattern, you will need to check the stitch repeat before deciding how many stitches to add or remove. That is, if the lace pattern is 10 stitches wide, there is no use in removing 17 stitches from the cast on because the pattern will then not fit, so go down 20 stitches instead.

Altering sleeve depth

If the measurement from armpit to shoulder is vastly different to that of your ideal garment then you will need to make some amendments here. Bear in mind that any rows you add or subtract here will need to be reflected in the sleeve cap shaping, otherwise the two will not fit together.

Look at the other sizes of the pattern. Do they offer a measurement that is closer in fit to the one that you wish to knit? If so, you may be able to use the increases or decreases suggested for the other size on both the sleeve cap and the top of the

garment. However, the stitch counts will not match if you do this, so depending on the complexity of the neckline, shoulders and collar, this may lead to more complex alterations being necessary.

Bust measurements

Measure around your actual bust to find out the amount of ease that you have in your ideal-fit garment. If your garment is 3in bigger than your bust size, you need to ensure that the garment you are going to knit is of a similar size.

Most patterns tell you how much ease is given in the pattern, and you should check the actual bust size of the garment rather than the number given 'to fit bust size' so that you can be sure you are making the right size. Compare this with the numbers you have written in your blank schematic and check that you are knitting the right size.

Alter length and width at the hem.   **Take care with sleeve caps.**   **Adjust the bust to fit you.**

2
INTERMEDIATE

About this
Pattern...

Yarn Make-Up
Piece of Beauty Aran Silkywool,
50% silk, 50% wool
Wraps per inch (WPI): 9

Yarn Alternatives
£ *Save:* Stylecraft, Life Aran

££ *Spend*: Sublime, Cashmere Merino
Silk Aran

£££ *Treat:* Cashmere oddments

Tension
Work 12 sts and 24 rows to measure
10 x 10cm, 4 x 4in, in st st using 6mm
(US10) needles.

Notions
6mm (US 10) circular needle,
80cm/32in long
6mm (US 10) circular needle,
40cm/16in long
4 stitch markers
1 removable marker or safety pin
2 stitch holders
50cm/0.5yd cotton print fabric
Sewing needle and thread

Pattern Notes
The cardigan is worked from top down
in one piece. The fabric panels are
sewn on at the end.

Flared · Cardigan

Flared shaping on the sleeves and fabric bands
make this a unique cardigan.

Size and yarn guide

To fit bust	26	30	34	38	42	46	50	in
	66	76	86.5	97	107	117	127	cm
Actual bust	28	32	36	40	44	48	52	in
	71	81.5	91.5	101.5	112	122	132	cm
Yarn needed								
Piece of Beauty Aran, Silkywool, 100g/ 125m/137yd, shade purple	4 skeins	5 skeins	5 skeins	6 skeins	6 skeins	7 skeins	7 skeins	
Total metres	500	625	625	750	750	875	875	
Total yards	548	685	685	822	822	959	959	

Pattern

With longer circular needle, cast on 52 (56, 56, 64, 64, 64, 68) sts.

Row 1 (RS): k11 (12, 12, 14, 14, 14, 15) for left front, pm, k9 for left sleeve, pm, k12 (14, 14, 18, 18, 18, 20) for back, pm, k9 for right sleeve, pm, k11 (12, 12, 14, 14, 14, 15) for right sleeve.

Row 2 (WS): P.

Row 3 (RS): *k to 1 st before m, yo, k1, sm, yo; rep from * three times more, k to end. 8 sts increased.

Row 4 (WS): P.

Rep Rows 3-4 14 (16, 19, 20, 21, 22, 22) times more. 172 (192, 216, 224, 248, 248, 252) sts.

Divide body and sleeves

Next row (RS): removing markers as you come to them, k to first m, place left sleeve sts on holder, cast on 0 (0, 0, 0, 4, 8, 12) sts for underarm, k to third m, place right sleeve sts on holder, cast on 0 (0, 0, 0, 4, 8, 12) sts for underarm, k to end. 94 (106, 118, 130, 142, 154, 166) sts.

Body

Work even in st st until body meas 59.5 (61, 62, 63.5, 65, 66, 66)cm/23.5 (24, 24.5, 25, 25.5, 26, 26)in, from back neck, ending with a p row.

Hem

P2 rows. K1 row. P1 row.

Cast off.

Sleeves

Place 39 (43, 49, 51, 53, 55, 55) held sts of one sleeve on shorter circular needle. Join yarn, pick up and K0 (0, 0, 0, 2, 4, 6) sts from underarm, pm for beg of round, pick up and K0 (0, 0, 0, 2, 4, 6) sts from underarm, K to end of round. 39 (43, 49, 51, 57, 63, 67) sts.

Work even in st st until sleeve meas 33 (33, 33, 34.5, 34.5, 34.5, 35.5)cm/13 (13, 13, 13.5, 13.5, 13.5, 14)in from underarm.

Cuff

At end of last round, remove m, turn work and begin working back-and-forth. Next row (WS): P 19 (21, 24, 25, 28, 31, 33), place removable m in next st, P to end.

Next row (RS): k to marked st, yo, k marked st, yo, k to end.

Next row (WS): P.

Rep last 2 rows 15 times more.

Hem

P2 rows. K1 row. P1 row. Cast off.

FINISHING

Weave in ends. From fabric, cut 2 pieces measuring 10cm/4in wide and 2.5cm /1in longer than the front edges of your cardigan. Fold all edges under 1cm/½in and press. Fold in half lengthwise and press. Pin to front edges, overlapping about 1cm/½in of the knitted material. Slip stitch in place and slip stitch short edges closed. Fasten with brooch.

To finish hems, turn under on the ridge made by the purl rows and slip stitch in place.

Summer
Halter

Make this in a cotton yarn for a fab summer top.

2
INTERMEDIATE

About this
Pattern...

Yarn
Rowan, Denim Cotton DK,
50g/93m/100yrd

Tension
Work 20 sts and 28 rows to measure
10 x 10cm/4 x 4in square in st st using
4.5mm (US7) needles.

Notions
A 16in 4.5mm (US7) circular needle
A 4.5mm (US7) needle

Pattern

NOTE for the larger bust sizes it might be preferable to overlap the triangles by picking up 5 stitches from behind the first triangle when knitting the second. This will provide some additional coverage and support.

Lower body

Using 4.5mm (US7) circular needle cast on [133, 145, 157, 169, 181, 193] sts. Place marker and join to begin working in the round, being careful not to twist. On the first row place another marker at [66, 72, 78, 84, 90, 96] stitches to represent the other side seam.

Knit the following 2 lace pattern rows until work measures 38 (39.5, 40.5, 42, 43, 44.5)cm/15 (15½, 16, 16½, 17, 17½)in.

Row 1: K1, *yo, ssk, k1, k2tog, yo, k1, repeat from * to the end.

Row 2: K2, *yo, sl2 as to knit, k1, pass the 2 slipped sts over, yo, k3, rep from *to last 5 sts, yo, sl2 as to knit, k1, pass the 2 slipped sts over, yo, k2

Now cast off [66, 72, 78, 84, 90, 96] sts between markers for the back and complete the 2 front sides separately as follows.

Front

Knit the first 33, 36, 39, 42, 45, 48 sts. Work from these stitches only to form the first triangle.

Work 3 rows in stocking stitch.

Continuing in stocking stitch and beginning on next RS row decrease 1 stitch at each end of the work every 4th row 5 times.

Then decrease 1 stitch at each end of every RS row until 4 stitches remain.

Work a 4 stitch i-cord for approx 25.5cm/10in. Cut yarn and pull through 4 sts and darn in end.

Return to front of halter neck and make a second triangle in the same way.

Size and yarn guide

To fit bust	30-32	34-36	38-40	42-44	46-48	50-52	in
	76-81	86.5-91	96-101	107-122	117-122	127-132	cm
Actual bust	32	36	40	44	48	52	in
	81	91	101	112	122	132	cm
Yarn	5	5	6	6	6	7	balls
Metreage	500	500	600	600	600	700	
Yardage	465	465	588	588	588	651	

2

INTERMEDIATE

About this
Pattern...

Yarn Alternatives
- **£ Save:** Sirdar Snuggly 4 ply
- **££ Spend:** Lorna's Laces, Shepherd Sock
- **£££ Treat:** Fyberspates, Sparkle Sock

Tension
Work 26 sts and 28 rows to equal
10 x 10cm/4 x 4in in stockinette
Work 32 sts and 28 rows to equal
10 x 10cm/4 x 4in over Cable A pattern

Notions
4.5mm (US 7) circular needle,
60cm/24in long
Tapestry needle
Cable needle
Stitch markers
25mm/1in grosgrain ribbon

Pattern Notes
As this pattern has some very large
cable crossings, you may prefer to use
a regular double-pointed needle as a
cable needle.

Cabled Top

This sleeveless cabled tank uses plant-dyed yarn
to make a statement.

Yoke
Cast on 76 (76, 84, 84, 92, 92,
100) sts. Do not join.
Set-up row (RS): K13 (13, 15, 15, 17, 17,
19) (Left Front), pm, k12 (Sleeve), pm, k26
(26, 30, 30, 34, 34, 38) (Back), pm, k12
(Sleeve), pm, k13 (13, 15, 15, 17, 17, 19)
(Right Front).
Next row (WS): Purl.
Inc row (RS): *K to 1 st before marker, kfb,
sl marker, kfb; rep from * three times more,
knit to end. 8 sts inc'd.
Rep the last 2 rows 31 (37, 40, 44, 48, 52, 55)
times more, until there are 90 (102, 112, 120,
132, 140, 150) sts in the Back section. Do not
turn at end of last row (RS). Join for working
in the round.

Cast ON

Divide body and sleeves
Next rnd (RS): K to first marker, cast off
all Sleeve sts between first and second
markers, k to third marker, cast off all Sleeve
sts between third and fourth markers, k to
end of rnd.
Next rnd: K across Front to cast-off section,
cast on 0 (0, 1, 3, 3, 5,6) sts for underarm,
pm for side 'seam', cast on 0 (0, 1, 3, 3, 5,
6) sts for underarm, k across Back to cast-off
section, cast on 0 (0, 1, 3, 3, 5, 6) sts for
underarm, pm for new beg of round, cast
on 0 (0, 1, 3, 3, 5, 6) sts for underarm, k
across Front and all the way around Body to
beg-of-rnd marker. 180 (204, 228, 252, 276,
300, 324) sts.

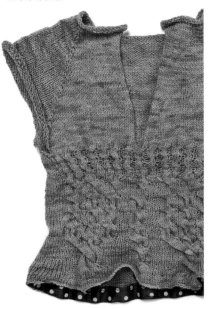

Stitch Patterns

Cable A

Worked over 6 sts

Rnds 1-3: Knit.

Rnd 4: *C6L; rep from * to end.

Rnds 5-7: Knit.

Rnd 8: *C6R; rep from * to end.

Rep Rnds 1-8.

Cable B

Worked over 12 sts

Rnds 1-5: Knit.

Rnd 6: C12L.

Rep Rnds 1-6.

Cable C

Worked over 36 sts

Rnds 1-5: Knit.

Rnd 6: (C12L) three times.

Rnds 7-30: Rep Rnds 1-6 four times.

Rnds 31-35: Knit.

Rnd 36: C36L.

Rnds 37-41: Knit.

Rnd 42: C36L.

C6L: Sl 3 sts to cable needle (cn) and hold to front of work, k3, k3 from cn.

C6R: Sl 2 sts to cable needle (cn) and hold to back, k3, k3 from cn.

C12L: Sl 6 sts to cable needle (cn) and hold to front, k6, k6 from cn.

C36L: Sl 18 sts to cable needle (cn) and hold to front, k18, k18 from cn.

Body

Set-up rnd 1: Work Rnd 1 of Cable A 15 (17, 19, 21, 23, 25, 27) times across 90 (102, 114, 126, 138, 150, 162) sts of Front, sl marker, knit across Back to end. Continue as set with Front sts in Cable A patt and Back in stockinette until you have worked 3 reps (18 rnds total) of Cable A.

Set-up rnd 2: K0 (0, 6, 6, 12, 12, 18) work Rnd 1 of Cable C over next 36 sts, k3 (9, 9, 15, 15, 21, 21), work Rnd 1 of Cable B over next 12 sts, k3 (9, 9, 15, 15, 21, 21), work Rnd 1 of Cable C over next 36 sts, k 0 (0, 6, 6, 12, 12, 18), sl marker, knit across Back to end.

Continue as set with Front sts in est cable patts and Back in stockinette until you have completed the 42 rnds of Cable C.

K 6 rnds, or to desired length.

Cast off.

Finishing

Weave in ends. Allow the stitches at the neck and around the sleeves to roll naturally. Sew the grosgrain ribbon to the inside of the bottom of the garment to prevent it from rolling. If you don't wish to use ribbon, you could work 8 rows of moss stitch, garter stitch or 2x2 rib at the bottom hem before casting off to prevent rolling.

Cable Chart A

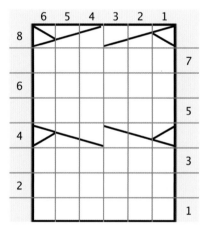

Cable Chart B

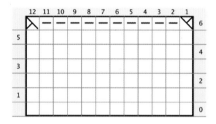

Cable Chart C

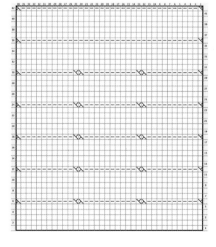

 knit

RS: Knit Stitch

WS: Purl Stitch

 c3 over 3 left

RS: sl3 to CN, hold to front, KS, K3 from CN

c3 over 3 right

RS: si3 to CN, hold to back, K3, K3 from CN

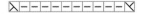 **c6 over 6 left**

RS: sl6 to CN, hold to front, k6, k6 from CN

c18 cover 18 left

RS: sl18 to CN, hold to front, k18, k18 from CN

V-Neck Vest

The deep rib and elegant v-neck make
this a stylish layering piece.

1

BEGINNER

About this
Pattern...

Yarn Make-up

Manos del Uruguay, Handspun
Multicolors (chunky), 100g/126m/
138yd, 100% wool

Yarn Alternatives

£ **Save:** Cascade Yarns, Cascade 128

££ **Spend:** Manos del Uruguay, Handspun

£££ **Treat:** Rowan, Scottish Aran Tweed

Tension

Work 14 sts and 20 rows to measure 10
x 10cm/4 x 4in over st st. using 5.5mm
(US9) needles.

Notions

One pair of 5.5mm (US9) needles
Stitch holder
Crochet hook
Tapestry needle

Back

Cast on 56 (62, 68, 74, 80,
86, 92) sts.
Row 1: p4, *k3, p3; rep from * to last 4
sts, k4.
Rep Row 1 until rib measures 24cm/9.5in.
Continue in st st until piece measures 31.5
(31.5, 33, 34.5, 35.5, 35.5, 37)cm/12.5
(12.5, 13, 13.5, 14, 14, 14.5)in from
cast-on edge, ending with a WS row.

Shape armholes

Cast off 2 (2, 3, 3, 4, 4, 5) sts at beg of next
2 rows. 52 (58, 62, 68, 72, 78, 82) sts.
Continue in st st until piece measures 49.5
(49.5, 52, 54.5, 56, 57, 60)cm/19.5 (19.5,
20.5, 21.5, 22, 22.5, 23.5)in from cast-on
edge. Cast off.

Front

Work as for Back until piece measures 34.5
(34.5, 35.5, 37, 38, 38, 39.5)cm/13.5 (13.5,
14, 14.5, 15, 15, 15.5)in from cast-on edge,
ending with a WS row.

Shape neck

Next row (RS): k26 (29, 31, 34, 36, 39, 41),
turn. Leave rem sts on holder.
Next row (WS): p2tog, purl to end—1 st
dec'd.
Next row (RS): knit.
Rep last 2 rows until 12 (12, 14, 15, 16, 18,
19) sts rem.
Work even, if necessary, until Front
measures same as Back to shoulder.

Cast ON

Cast off.
Rejoin yarn to rem sts with RS facing
and complete to match first side,
reversing shaping.

Finishing

Join shoulder and side seams.
Work 1 round of double crochet around
neckline and armholes.
Weave in ends.

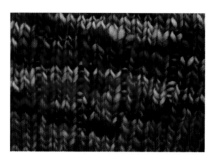

Size and yarn guide

To fit bust	30-31	32-35	36-38	39-41	42-45	46-48	49-52	in
	76-78.5	81.5-90	91.5-96	99-104	106.5-114.	116.5-122	124.5-132	cm
Actual bust	31	34	37½	41	44.5	48	51.5	in
	78.5	86.5	95	104	113	122	131	cm
Yarn needed								
Jaeger, Extra Fine Merino Chunky 50g/63m/69yd	3 skeins	3 skeins	3 skeins	4 skeins	4 skeins	4 skeins	5 skeins	
Total metres	378	378	378	504	504	504	630	
Total yards	414	414	414	552	552	552	690	

SCHEMATIC

15 (16.5, 17.75, 19.5, 20.5, 22, 23.5)in
38 (42, 45, 49.5, 52, 56, 59.5)cm

7 (7, 7.5, 8, 8, 8.5, 9)in
18 (18, 19, 20.5, 20.5, 21.5, 23)cm

12.5 (12.5, 13, 13.5, 14, 14, 14.5)in
31.5 (31.5, 33, 34.5, 35.5, 35.5, 37)cm

15.5 (17, 19, 20.5, 22.25, 24, 25.75)in
39.5 (43, 48.5, 51, 56.5, 61, 65.5)cm

2
INTERMEDIATE

Caterpillar Cardi

Flared shaping on the sleeves and fabric bands make this a unique cardigan.

About this Pattern...

Skills Used

Stocking Stitch
Reverse Stocking Stitch
Decreasing

Yarn Alternatives

£ **Save:** Sirdar, Tweedie chunky

££ **Spend:** Rowan, Cocoo

£££ **Treat:** Cashmere oddments

Yarn Used

Rowan Kaffe Fassett colourscape chunky

Tension

14 stitches and 20 rows to 10cm.

Pattern Notes

This is a raglan sweater, knitted from the bottom up.

Making Up

Join sleeve seams. If you want to stretch out the rib pattern and press it flat, the body and sleeves will be longer. To leave it stretchy, as shown, do not press or block.

Stitch Pattern

Work alternate ridges of 4 rows stocking stitch followed by 4 rows reverse stocking stitch. Each 4 rows is 1 ridge.

Body

Cast on 124 (138, 152, 166, 180, 194) stitches and work in stitch pattern until 20 (22, 24, 26, 28, 30) ridges have been completed. Move body to spare needles or waste yarn.

Arms (make 2 alike)

Cast on 40 (50, 60, 70, 80, 90) stitches and work in caterpillar pattern until 30 (32, 33, 34, 35, 36) ridges have been completed. Move each arm to spare needles or waste yarn.

Cast ON

Size and Yarn Amount

Sizes	30/32	34/36	38/40	42/44	46/48	50/52	UK
Actual Bust	77.5	87.5	97.5	107.5	117.5	127.5	cm
	31	35	39	43	47	51	in
Actual length to shoulder	59	64.5	68	73.5	79	82.5	cm
	24	26	27	29	32	33	in
Actual Sleeve Length	37	41	43	47	51	53	cm
	15	17	19	21	23	25	in
Yarn (Skeins)	3	4	4	5	6	6	
Total Metres	480	640	640	800	800	960	
Total Yards	525	700	700	875	875	1050	

Join body and arms

Rejoin yarn to body and ensuring that the
caterpillar pattern remains consistent, knit
the first 40 (45, 50, 55, 60, 65) stitches,
then knit the stitches from one of the arms,
knit another 62 (67, 72, 77, 82, 87) stitches
from the body, then the stitches from the
other arm and finally the last 22 (26, 30,
34, 38, 42) stitches from the body. This
makes the asymmetrical shape.

Top of cardi

Work remaining 3 rows of ridge pattern,
placing marker at the beginning and end
of both sleeves to mark where the raglan
decreases need to be.

Continue working in the caterpillar pattern
as set, decreasing stitches before and after
each marker on every right-side row until
2 stitches remain on narrowest part of the
front. Work straight without decreases for 3
ridges for the collar.

Cast off.

Top Tip

Using the circular needle will
make the first few rows of the
raglan section easier to manage
when you have lots of stitches
on the needle.

*This is a raglan sweater, knitted
from the bottom up, using alternate
ridges of stocking and reverse
stocking stitch.*

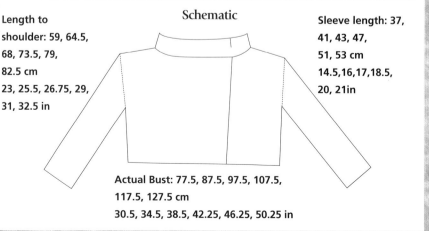

Length to shoulder: 59, 64.5, 68, 73.5, 79, 82.5 cm
23, 25.5, 26.75, 29, 31, 32.5 in

Schematic

Sleeve length: 37, 41, 43, 47, 51, 53 cm
14.5, 16, 17, 18.5, 20, 21in

Actual Bust: 77.5, 87.5, 97.5, 107.5, 117.5, 127.5 cm
30.5, 34.5, 38.5, 42.25, 46.25, 50.25 in

Kimono

A warm and cosy jacket inspired by Noro yarn
and Japanese kimonos.

2

INTERMEDIATE

About this Pattern...

Yarn

MC: Noro Silk Garden, shade 211
CC: Noro Cash Iroha, shade 2

Yarn Content

MC: 45% Silk, 45% Mohair,
10% Lambswool
CC: 40% Silk, 30% Lambswool,
20% Cashmere, 10% Nylon

Yarn Alternatives

£ **Save:** Cygnet, Wool Rich Aran

££ **Spend:** Rowan, Pure Wool Aran

£££ **Treat:** Lorna's Laces, Shepherd

Tension

Work 18 sts and 24 rows to measure
10 x 10cm/4 x 4in in st st using 5mm
(U87) needles

Notions

5mm (US8) knitting needles
5mm (US8) 100cm circular needle
5mm DPNs (if required for I-cord ties)
3 large buttons
1 medium button

The skirt

In MC, cast on 54, (60, 64, 68,
74, 78, 82, 88) stitches and work in
stocking stitch for 60, (70, 78, 88,
98, 108, 118, 128) rows, ending with WS
row.

Insert dart as follows

Row 1 Knit to the last 6 stitches, W&T (5
stitches remain on needle)
Row 2 & all other WS rows Purl
Rows 3, 5, 7, 9 & 11 Knit to 6 stitches
before last wrapped stitch, W&T.
Row 12 Purl, picking up the wrapped
stitches as you go along.
Rows 13-24 Repeat rows 1-12
Continue in st sti and work a further 40,
[44, 46, 50, 52, 56, 58, 62] rows.

This will bring you to the centre of back.
Work another dart as before. Note that it
looks better if you can do rows 1 – 12 in
one colour and then start a new ball of
yarn in the same colour so that the dart is
essentially in the same colour.
Continue in stocking stitch for another 40,
[44, 46, 50, 52, 56, 58, 62] rows.

Pattern Note

The band is designed to fit comfortably under your chest and can be pulled as tight
or loose as you wish. If you do not like the buttons, or want to have the option of
changing the tightness, you can knit I-cord ties (four stitches) and place where the
buttons are on the band (you will still require a medium size button for inside).
The size charts below are split so have the flexibility to make a larger top section or
skirt, depending on your requirements. If you have a larger skirt than top, you will
need to add some short rows into the waistband to accommodate the different sizing.
Likewise, if you choose to knit a larger top than skirt you will also need to do this. It is
suggested that you do not go up/down more than one size.

Size and yarn guide

Size	1	2	3	4	5	6	7	8	
To fit bust	76-81	86-91	96-101	107-112	117-122	127-132	137-142	147-152	cm
	30-32	34-36	38-40	42-44	46-48	50-52	54-56	58-60	in
Actual bust	81	91	101	112	122	132	142	152	cm
	32	36	40	44	48	52	56	60	in
Waist	56-61	66-71	76-81	84-91	95-102	107-112	117-122	127-132	cm
	22-24	26-28	30-32	34-36	38-40	42-44	46-48	50-52	in
Finished waist	81	94	104	114	124	135	147	157	cm
	32	37	41	45	49	53	58	62	in
Lower hips	81-86	91-96	101-107	112-117	122-127	132-137	142-147	152-157	cm
	32-34	36-38	40-42	44-46	48-50	52054	56-58	60-62	in
Finished lower hips	91	101	112	122	132	142	152	168	cm
	36	40	44	48	52	58	62	66	in
Yarn needed									
MC: Noro Silk Garden, 50g/100m/110yd, shade 211	7 balls	8 balls	9 balls	10 balls	11 balls	12 balls	13 balls	14 balls	
Total metres	700	800	900	1,000	1,100	1,200	1,300	1,400	
Total yards	770	880	990	1,100	1,210	1,320	1,430	1,540	
CC: Noro, Cash Iroha, 50g/133m/145yd, shade 2	3 balls	3 balls	3 balls	3 balls	4 balls	4 balls	4 balls	4 balls	
Total metres	399	399	399	399	532	532	532	532	
Total yards	435	435	435	435	580	580	580	580	

Work another dart as before.
Continue in stocking stitch for another 60, [70, 78, 88, 98, 108, 118, 128] rows and then cast off.

Waist band

Waistband without darts (no difference in sizing between skirt and main section):
In CC, cast on 24, [26, 26, 26, 28, 28, 28, 28] stitches and work in garter stitch for 200, [226, 248, 274, 300, 326, 352, 378] rows. Cast off.
Waistband with darts (skirt one size larger than main section, given below as size 1-2, size 2-3, size 3-4, size 4-5, size 5-6,

size 6-7, size 7-8): In CC, cast on 24, [26, 26, 26, 28, 28, 28, 28] stitches and work in garter stitch for 60, [70, 78, 88, 98, 108] rows. Insert dart as follows: Row 1, 3, 5 Knit to the last 4 stitches.

W&T
Rows 2 & 4 Knit
Row 6 Knit picking up all wrapped stitches.
Rows 7 & 8 Knit (whole row)
Row 9, 11, 13 Knit to the last 4 stitches, W&T

Rows 10&12 Knit
Row 14 Knit, picking up all wrapped stitches.

Work for another 80, [86, 92, 98, 104, 110, 136] rows and then insert another dart as before. Work for another 60, [70, 78, 88, 98, 108] rows and then cast off.

Back

Cast on 58 [60, 62, 62, 64, 64, 64, 64] stitches and work 14 [14, 16, 16, 16, 18,18, 18] rows in stocking stitch.

Decrease 1 stitch at the end of each RS (knit) row and 1 at the start of each WS (purl) row for 8, [8, 10, 10, 12, 12, 12, 12] rows. Decrease 2 stitches as set for two more rows. 12, [12, 12, 14, 16, 16, 16, 16] stitches cast off, 46 [48, 48, 48, 48, 48, 48, 48] stitches remain.

Knit 28, [34, 36, 38, 40, 42, 48, 54] rows in stocking stitch.

Increase 1 stitch at the end of each RS (knit) row and 1 at the start of each WS (purl) row for 8, [8, 10, 10, 12, 12, 12, 12] rows. Increase 2 stitches as set for two more rows. 12, [12, 12, 14, 16,

16, 16, 16, 16] stitches cast on. You are back to original cast on of 58 [60, 62, 62, 64, 64, 64, 64] stitches. Work a further 14 [14, 16, 16, 16, 18, 18, 18] rows in st st and then cast off.

Front pieces
Left piece

Cast on 58, [60, 62, 62, 62, 64, 64, 64] stitches and work for 14, [14, 16, 16, 16, 18, 18, 18] rows in stocking stitch.

Size 1

52 stitches over 46 rows.

Decrease 2 stitches at the end of each RS (knit) row and start of each WS (purl) row for 6 rows, and then 1 as set for 40 rows. 6 stitches remain. Cast off.

Sizes 2

54 stitches over 56 rows.

Decrease 2 stitches at the end of each RS (knit) row and start of each WS (purl) row for 2 row and start of each WS (purl) row

for 2 rows, and then at the end of each RS (knit) row start of each WS (purl) row for 54 rows.6 stitches remain. Cast off.

Size 3

56 stitches over 62 rows.

Decrease 1 stitch at the end of each RS (knit) row for 12 rows only (6 stitches decreased) and then at the end of each RS (knit) row start of each WS (purl) row for 50 rows.

6 stitches remain. Cast off.

Size 4

56 stitches over 72 rows.

Decrease 1 stitch at the end of each RS (knit) row for 32 rows only (16 stitches decreased) and then at the end of each RS (knit) row start of each WS (purl) row for 40 rows.

6 stitches remain. Cast off.

Size 5

58 stitches over 82 rows.

Decrease 1 stitch at the end of each RS (knit) row for 52 rows only (26 stitches decreased) and then at the end of each RS (knit) row start of each WS (purl) row for 30 rows.

6 stitches remain. Cast off.

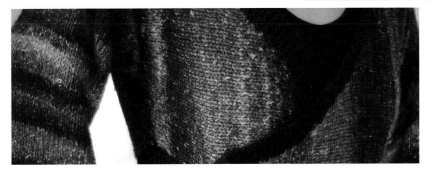

Size 8

58 stitches over 110 rows.
Decrease 1 stitch at the end of each RS (knit) row for 108 rows only (54 stitches decreased) and then at the end of each RS (knit) row start of each WS (purl) row for 2 rows.
6 stitches remain. Cast off.

Right piece

As above, except work your decreases at the start of each RS (knit row) and at the end of each WS (purl) row.

Sleeves

These are essentially large rectangles that are then folded in two, worked in stocking stitch, ending with eight rows in garter stitch with contrasting yarn.
Cast on 74, [76, 78, 80, 82, 84, 88, 90] stitches in MC and work for 98, [100, 104, 108, 110, 114, 116, 120] rows, ending with a WS row.
Join CC at start of next row and work for 8 rows in garter stitch.
Cast Off.

Finishing

Block all pieces. You may wish to use another yarn, such as Cascade 220 or similar, to sew the garment together as Noro splits easily.
First join the shoulder sections of the front pieces and back. Join sleeves and then sew along the underside of the sleeves and main body of the front and back pieces. Join waistband to main section, and finally join the skirt to the waistband.

Size 6

58 stitches over 90 rows.
Decrease 1 stitch at the end of each RS (knit) row for 68 rows only (34 stitches decreased) and then at the end of each RS (knit) row start of each WS (purl) row for 22 rows.
6 stitches remain. Cast off.

Size 7

58 stitches over 100 rows.
Decrease 1 stitch at the end of each RS (knit) row for 88 rows only (44 stitches decreased) and then at the end of each RS (knit) row start of each WS (purl) row for 12 rows.
6 stitches remain. Cast off.

Borders

Bottom border

With a long circular needle, pick up and knit every 2 out of 3 stitches from the skirt. Approximately 272, [298, 320, 346, 372, 398, 424, 450] stitches on needles.
Knit 8 rows in garter stitch.
Cast off.

Main border

Pick up and knit every 2 out of 3 stitches starting at the bottom left-hand corner of the skirt, work your way up the left-hand side, across the neck and back down the right-hand side to the bottom corner of the right-hand side of the skirt. Approximately 384, {426, 456, 490, 532, 566, 600, 638] stitches on needles.
When you get to the waistband (on both sides), make sure that you leave gaps in suitable places for buttonholes.
You create a buttonhole by casting on 3 (or 4, depending on size of button) stitches instead of picking up 3 (or 4 stitches).
You will need to create 3 buttonholes on the left-hand side of the waistband and one (or more, depending on your requirements) on the right hand side.

Once you have picked up all your stitches, knit 8 rows in garter stitch and then cast off on a RS row.

Sew buttons in place.
Block again if required.

Grey Vest

Clever, sexy and smart, this deep V-neck tank top works well with a classic blouse.

About this
Pattern...

Yarn

Jaeger, Extra Fine Merino Aran, 100% merino wool

Yarn Alternatives

£   **Save:** Cygnet, Wool Rich Aran

££   **Spend:** Rowan, Pure Wool Aran

£££   **Treat:** Lorna's Laces, Shepherd

Tension

Work 18 sts and 24 rows to measure 10 x 10cm/4 x 4in in st st using 4.5mm (US7) needles

Notions

One pair 4mm (US6) needles
 (if required)
One pair 4.5mm (US7) needles
One 4mm (US6) 60cm circular needle
Set of 4mm (US6) DPNs
Stitch holder

Pattern

Back

Using smaller needles cast on 62 (66, 70, 74, 78, 82, 86, 90, 94, 98, 102) sts.
Work 10 rows in k1, p1 rib.
Change to st st and work straight until piece measures 9 (10, 10, 11.5, 11.5, 12.5, 12.5, 14, 14, 15.5, 15.5)cm/3.5 (4, 4, 4.5, 4.5, 5, 5, 5.5, 5.5, 6, 6)in.

Waist shaping

Next row (RS): k1, k2tog, k to last 3 sts, ssk, k1. Repeat this waist shaping every 6 rows twice more.
Work straight in st st until work measures 21.5 (23, 23. 24, 24, 25.5, 25.5, 26.5, 26.5, 28, 28)cm/8.5 (9, 9, 9.5, 9.5, 10, 10, 10.5, 10.5, 11, 11)in.

Next row: k1, m1r, k to last st, m1l. Repeat this waist shaping every 6 rows twice more.

Work straight in st st until piece measures 34 (35.5, 35.5, 37, 37, 38, 38, 39.5. 39.5, 40.5, 40.5)cm/13.5 (14, 14, 14.5, 14.5, 15, 15, 15.5, 15.5, 16, 16)in.

Shape armholes

Cast off 3 sts at the beginning of the next 4 rows.
Work straight in st st until armhole measures 19 (20.5, 20.5, 21.5, 21.5, 23, 23, 24, 24, 25.5, 25.5)cm/7.5 (8, 8, 8.5, 8.5, 9, 9, 9.5, 9.5, 10, 10)in.

Shape, shoulders and neck

Work 16 (16, 17, 17, 18, 18, 20, 20, 22, 22) sts, cast off to last 16 (16, 17, 17, 18, 18, 20, 20, 22, 22) sts.
Next row: cast off 16 (16, 17, 17, 18, 18, 20, 20, 22, 22) sts.
Rejoin yarn to opposite side and cast off all sts.

Front

Work as for back until piece measures 15 (15, 15, 15, 18, 18, 18, 18, 20.5, 20.5, 20.5)cm/6 (6, 6, 6, 7, 7, 7, 7, 8, 8, 8)in.

Shape left neck

Next row (RS) work to centre st and turn. Working left neck sts only, and with right neck sts on holder, sl 1, p to end. Slipped st will form chain selvedge for picking up neckline.

Next row: k to last 3 sts, ssk, k1.
Repeat this decrease row every 4th row until 16 (16, 17, 17, 18, 18, 20, 20, 22, 22) sts remain.

Work straight until piece measures until armhole measures 19 (20.5, 20.5, 21.5, 21.5, 23, 23, 24, 24, 25.5, 25.5)cm/7.5 (8, 8, 8.5, 8.5, 9, 9, 9.5, 9.5, 10, 10)in.

Cast off all sts.

Shape right neck

Return right neck sts to working needles.
Beginning with a RS row, sl 1, ktog,
k to end.
Repeat this decrease row every 4th row
until 16 (16, 17, 17, 18, 18, 20, 20, 22, 22)
sts remain.
Work straight until armhole measures 19
(20.5, 20.5, 21.5, 21.5, 23, 23, 24, 24,
25.5, 25.5)cm/7.5 (8, 8, 8.5, 8.5, 9, 9, 9.5,
9.5, 10, 10)in.
Cast off all sts.

Finishing

Sew shoulders and side seams
together.

Neck cable

From bottom of V up right neck to centre
of back, pick up sts at this rate: 2 picked up
sts in every 3 cast off sts, 1 picked up st in
every slipped st of chain selvedge.

Cast on 9 sts using cable cast-on.
Row 1 and all WS rows p8, p2tog.
Rows 2, 4 and 8 k9.
Row 6 k1, C8B.
Continue working the cable band in this
fashion until 4 picked-up sts remain.

Shape Bottom of V

Row 1 p8, p2tog.
Row 2 k3, W&T.
Row 3 p2, p2tog.
Row 4 k6, W&T.
Row 5 p5, p2tog.
Row 6 k.
Cast off.

From centre back along left side down to
bottom of V, pick up sts as before. Cast on
9 sts using cable cast-on.

Row 1 p8, p2tog.
Row 2 k6, W&T.
Row 3 p5, p2tog.
Row 4 k3, W&T.
Row 5 p2, p2tog.
Row 6 k.

Matching first C8B row to position of
last C8B row on right side, work in cable
pattern until all picked up sts have been
knitted in.
Cast off.

Sew neckband together at back of neck and
bottom of V.

Armhole ribbing

Pick up all sts around armhole and work
in k1, p1 rib for 2.5cm/1in. If necessary,
decrease 1 st at end of first round to
achieve even number of sts.
Cast off all sts.

Charts

Neck Cable

8	ǀ	ǀ	ǀ	ǀ	ǀ	ǀ	ǀ	ǀ		
	⅄	ǀ	ǀ	ǀ	ǀ	ǀ	ǀ	ǀ	ǀ	7
6	ǀ									
	⅄	ǀ	ǀ	ǀ	ǀ	ǀ	ǀ	ǀ	ǀ	5
4	ǀ	ǀ	ǀ	ǀ	ǀ	ǀ	ǀ	ǀ		
	⅄	ǀ	ǀ	ǀ	ǀ	ǀ	ǀ	ǀ	ǀ	3
2	ǀ	ǀ	ǀ	ǀ	ǀ	ǀ	ǀ	ǀ		
	⅄	ǀ	ǀ	ǀ	ǀ	ǀ	ǀ	ǀ	ǀ	1

Note:
**All odd-numbered rows
are WS, all even-numbered
rows are RS**

Key

	K on RS, p on WS.
	p last st of edging tog with picked-up st in necline on WS
	C8B

Size and yarn guide

To fit bust	30	32	34	36	38	40	42	44	46	48	50	in
	76	81	86.5	91.5	96.5	101.5	107	112	117	122	127	cm
Actual bust	30	32	34	36	38	40	42	44	46	48	50	in
	76	81	86.5	91.5	96.5	101.5	107	112	117	122	127	cm
Yarn needed												
Jaeger, Extra Fine Merino Aran, 50g/ 87m/95yd, shade	5 balls	5 balls	6 balls	6 balls	7 balls	7 balls	8 balls	8 balls	9 balls	9 balls	10 balls	
Total metres	435	435	522	522	609	609	697	697	783	783	870	
Total yards	475	475	570	570	665	665	760	760	855	855	950	

1

About this Pattern...

Skills Used

Increasing and decreasing

Pick up and knit

Knitting in rows

Seaming

Yarn Used

Wollmeise 100% Merino Superwash •

100% merino • 150g/526m/575yd

• WPI 14

Colour: Igor

Yarn Alternatives

£ **Save:** Jamieson Smith 2ply
Jumper Weight

££ **Spend:** Rowan Cashcotton 4ply

£££ **Treat:** Fyberspates Scrumptious Sock

Tension

Work 28sts and 36 rows in Stocking stitch to measure 10 x 10cm/4 x 4in using 3mm (US 2.5) needles, or size required to obtain tension.

Notions

A pair of 2.5mm (US 1.5) knitting needles

A pair of 3mm (US 2.5) knitting needles

A set of four 2.5mm (US 1.5) double-pointed needles or 40cm circular needle

Stitch holder or spare yarn

Tapestry Needle

Women's Sweater

Substitute the variegated colourway for a bright, solid colour for a sexy and chic garment.

Back

Cast on 115 (121: 127: 136: 142: 148: 157: 163: 169: 178) sts using 2.5mm (US 1.5) needles.

Row 1 (RS): K3, *p1 k2; rep from * to last stitch, k1.

Row 2 (WS): P3, *k1, p2; rep from * to last stitch, p1.

Repeat these 2 rows 6 times, or until the rib measures 2.5cm/1in.

Change to 3mm (US 2.5) needles.

Work 8 rows in st st.

*Next Row (RS): K1, k2tog, knit to last 3 sts, ssk, k1.

Work 7 rows in st st.

Repeat from * twice more. 109 (115: 121: 130: 136: 142: 151: 157: 163: 172) sts.

Work 20 rows in st st, ending with a Ws row.

Cast ON

**Next Row (RS): K1, m1, knit to last st, m1, k1.

Work 9 rows in st st.

Size & yarn amount

To fit bust	76	81.5	86.5	91.5	96.5	100	105	112	117	127	cm
	30	32	34	36	38	40	42	44	46	50	in
Finished bust	81.5	86.5	91.5	96.5	100	105	112	117	127	132	cm
	32	34	36	38	40	42	44	46	48	50	in
Sleeve seam	56	57	58.5	58.5	58.5	59.5	61	61	62	63.5	cm
	22	22½	23	23	23	23½	24	24	24½	25	in
Length	49	49	49	50.5	50.5	51	51	51	51.5	51.5	balls
	19½	19½	19½	20	20	20¼	20¼	20¼	20½	20½	_
Yarn	3	3	3	3	3	3	3	3	4	4	_
Total yards	1725	1725	1725	1725	1725	1725	1725	1725	2300	2300	_

Repeat from ** twice more. 115 (121: 127: 136: 142: 148: 157: 163: 169: 178) sts.

Work in St st until piece measures 30cm/12in or desired length from underarm, ending with a WS row.

Armhole shaping

Cast off 6 (6: 7: 8: 9: 9: 10: 11: 12: 14) sts at beginning of next 2 rows.

Dec 1 st at each end of every RS row 6 (6: 6: 7: 8: 9: 11: 11: 11: 12) times. 91 (97: 101: 106: 108: 112: 115: 119: 123: 126) sts.

*** Work in St st until piece measures 19 (19: 19: 20.5: 20.5: 21: 21: 21: 21.5: 21.5) cm/7.5 (7.5: 7.5: 8: 8: 8.25: 8.25: 8.25: 8.5: 8.5)in from start of armhole shaping, ending with a WS row.

Shape shoulders

Next Row (RS): Cast off 9 (10: 10: 10: 10: 8: 8: 9: 9: 9) sts, knit to end.

Next Row (WS): Cast off 9 (10: 10: 10: 10: 8: 8: 9: 9: 9) sts, purl until there are 18 (20: 20: 20: 20: 24: 24: 27: 27: 27) sts remaining and place them on a stitch holder. Turn.

Next Row (RS): Cast off 37 (37: 41: 46: 48: 48: 51: 47: 51: 54) sts, k to end.

Cast off 9 (10: 10: 10: 10: 8: 8: 9: 9: 9) sts at beg of every WS row until all sts have been cast off.

With WS facing, rejoin yarn to other side:

Next Row (WS): Purl.

Cast off 9 (10: 10: 10: 10: 8: 8: 9: 9: 9) sts at beg of every RS row until all sts have been cast off.

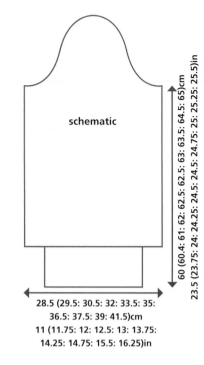

schematic

60 (60.4: 61: 62: 62.5: 62.5: 63: 63.5: 64.5: 65)cm
23.5 (23.75: 24: 24.25: 24.5: 24.5: 24.75: 25: 25.25: 25.5)in

28.5 (29.5: 30.5: 32: 33.5: 35: 36.5: 37.5: 39: 41.5)cm
11 (11.75: 12: 12.5: 13: 13.75: 14.25: 14.75: 15.5: 16.25)in

13.5 (13.5: 14.5: 16.5: 17.5: 17.5: 18.5: 17.5: 18.5: 19.5)cm
5.25 (5.25: 5.75: 6.5: 6.75: 6.75: 7.25: 6.75: 7.25: 7.75)in

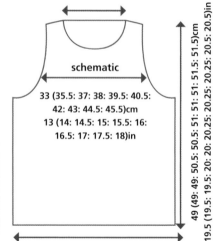

schematic

33 (35.5: 37: 38: 39.5: 40.5: 42: 43: 44.5: 45.5)cm
13 (14: 14.5: 15: 15.5: 16: 16.5: 17: 17.5: 18)in

49 (49: 49: 50.5: 50.5: 51: 51: 51: 51.5: 51.5)cm
19.5 (19.5: 19.5: 20: 20: 20.25: 20.25: 20.25: 20.5: 20.5)in

40.5 (43: 45.5: 48: 51: 53: 56: 58.5: 61: 63.5)cm
16 (17: 18: 19: 20: 21: 22: 23: 24: 25)in

Front

Work as Back to ***.

Work in St st until armhole measures 10.75 (10.75: 10.75: 11.5: 11.5: 11.5: 11.5: 11.5: 11.5: 11.5)cm or 4.25 (4.25: 4.25: 4.5: 4.5: 4.5: 4.5: 4.5: 4.5: 4.5) in ending with a WS row.

Knit 38 (41: 41: 41: 41: 43: 43: 47: 47: 47) sts and place on holder. Cast off centre 15 (15: 19: 24: 26: 26: 29: 25: 29: 32) sts, knit to end.

Dec 1 st at neck edge on next 6 rows, then every following alt row 5 times.

Work in St st until armhole measures 19 (19: 19: 20.5: 20.5: 21: 21: 21: 21.5: 21.5)cm or 7.5 (7.5: 7.5: 8: 8: 8.25: 8.25: 8: 8.5: 8.5)in from start of armhole shaping, ending with a WS row.

Shape shoulders

Cast off 9 (10: 10: 10: 10: 8: 8: 9: 9: 9) sts at beg of every WS row until all sts have been cast off.

Rejoin yarn to other side with WS facing and work as for first side. For shoulders cast off 9 (10: 10: 10: 10: 8: 8: 9: 9: 9) sts at beg of every RS row until all sts have been cast off.

Sleeves

Cast on 78 (82: 84: 88: 92: 96: 100: 104: 108: 114) sts using 3mm (US 2.5) needles.

Work in St st until work measures 42 (42.5: 43: 44: 44.5: 44.5: 45: 45.5: 46.5: 47)cm or 16.5 (16.75: 17: 17.25: 17.5: 17.5: 17.75: 18: 18.25: 18.5)in ending with a WS row.

Shape sleeve cap

Cast off 6 (6: 7: 8: 9: 9: 10: 11: 12: 14) sts at beg next 2 rows.

Dec 1 st at each end of the next 0 (4: 4: 2: 2: 4: 6: 8: 8: 8) rows.

Dec 1 st at each end of every RS row 15 (13: 13: 16: 17: 17: 16: 15: 16: 17) times.

Decrease 1 st each end of the next 8 rows.

Cast off remaining 20 sts.

Cuff

The cuffs are worked with significant negative ease, so it's best to try it on your arm as you go to ensure a comfortable, but snug, fit.

Using 2.5mm (US 1.5) needles, pick up 78 (82: 84: 88: 92: 96: 100: 104: 114) sts

114) sts along original edge.

K1, *k2tog; repeat from * to last st, k1.

Row 1 (WS): *P2, k1; rep from * to end.

Row 2 (RS): *P1, k2; rep from * to end.

Continue the cuffs in pattern, decreasing 1 st at each end every 6th row 2 times, then every 8th row 5 times.

Work 8 rows and cast off.

Finishing

Weave in ends and block.

Sew cuffs together using mattress stitch.

Seam Front, Back and Sleeves.

Collar

Using 2.5mm (US 1.5) circular needle or DPNs, pick up 15 (15: 19: 24: 26: 26: 29: 25: 29: 32) across front of the neckline, 22 (22: 22: 24: 24: 26: 26: 26: 27: 27) sts up left front, 37 (37: 42: 45: 49: 48: 51: 46: 52: 55) sts along Back and 22 (22: 22: 24: 24: 26: 26: 26: 27: 27) sts down right front.

Work in a k2 p1 rib for 2.5cm/1in.

Cast off.

Weave in ends.

Menswear

Try your hand at the projects in this section and create stylish and comfortable menswear, from a cosy scarf, to a classic button-down cardigan and woolly warm mittens.

Men's Mittens

Who says men can't wear bright colours?
These mitts make a strong statement but aren't girly!

2

INTERMEDIATE

About this
Pattern...

Skills Used

Knitting in the round
Stranded colourwork
Working from a chart
Pick up and knit
Yarn Over

Yarn

Schachenmayr Nomotta Favorit,
35% cotton, 35% acrylic, 30% viscose,
50g/123m/135yd, WPI 14
MC: 30 (red), 2 balls
CC: 56 (blue), 1 ball

Yarn Alternatives

£ **Save:** Sirdar Calico Cotton

££ **Spend:** Drops Merino Extra Fine

£££ **Treat:** Rowan Wool Cotton

Tension

For smallest size: 21sts and 32 rows to
10 x 10cm/4 x 4in in stocking stitch.
For largest size: 19.5 sts and 32 rows
to 10 x 10cm/4 x 4in in stocking stitch.

Notions

For smallest size: 2.5mm and 3mm (US
1.5 and 2.5) double-pointed needles
For largest size: 3mm and 3.5mm (US
2.5 and 4) double-pointed needles
Tapestry needle
Safety pin or stitch holders

Measurements

Small (Large)
18cm/7in (20cm/8in) hand
circumference, above crook of thumb.
28cm/11in (30cm/12in) long

Primary shades of red
and blue create a bold
contrast while the roomy fit
allows plenty of movement.

Cast ON

With MC and smallest needles, cast on
48 sts.
Divide sts evenly over needles and join to
work in the rnd.

Cuff

Work in k2, p2 rib for 15 rnds.
Switch to largest needles and knit 1 rnd.
Join CC and work chart (all stitches are
worked in stocking st).
After chart is complete, cut CC and secure
thread on inside of mitt.
Continuing with MC, knit 6 rnds.

Begin thumb gusset

For Left Mitten Only

Rnd 1: K2, yo, k8, yo, knit to end.
Rnd 2 and all even rnds: Knit.
Rnd 3: K3, yo, k8, yo, knit to end.
Rnd 5: K4, yo, k8, yo, knit to end.
Rnd 7: K5, yo, k8, yo, knit to end.
Rnd 9: K6, move next 8 sts to stitch holder,
cast on 2 sts, knit to end.
Rnd 11: K5, ssk, k2tog, knit to end.
48 sts remain.

For Right Mitten Only

Rnd 1: Knit to last 10 sts, yo, k8, yo, k2.

Rnd 2 and all even rnds: Knit.

Rnd 3: Knit to last 11 sts, yo, k8, yo, k3.

Rnd 5: Knit to last 12 sts, yo, k8, yo, k4.

Rnd 7: Knit to last 13 sts, yo, k8, yo, k5.

Rnd 9: Knit to last 14 sts, move next 8 sts to stitch holder, cast on 2 sts, k6.

Rnd 11: Knit to last 9 sts, ssk, k2tog, k5. 48 sts remain.

On both mittens, knit even in stocking st until mitten measures 3cm/1¼in shorter than desired total length.

Begin decreases

Next Rnd: *K9, k2tog, k1, place marker, k1, ssk, k9, place marker; rep from * once more.

Next Rnd: *K to 3 sts before next marker, k2tog, k1, slip marker (sm), k1, ssk, knit to next marker, sm; rep from * once more.

Rep last rnd eight times more. 8 sts remain.

Cut yarn, leaving 20cm/8in tail.

With tapestry needle, pull tail through remaining stitches.

Weave in ends.

Thumb

With MC and largest needles, pick up and knit 8 held thumb sts, and pick up and knit 10 sts around thumb gap (18 sts total).

Work even in stocking st until thumb measures desired total length of thumb.

Cut yarn, leaving 20cm/7.87 in tail.

With tapestry needle, pull tail through remaining stitches.

Weave in ends.

Colourwork chart

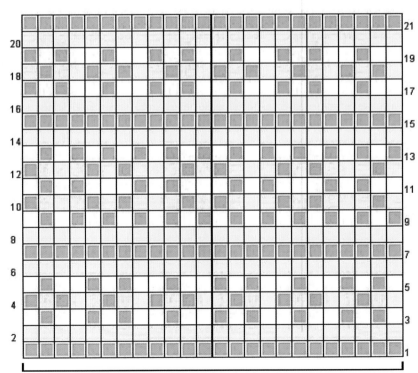

Work 2 times total

Chart Key

☐ K with MC   ▨ K with CC

2

INTERMEDIATE

Shawl-Collar Sweater

This stylish men's sweater is the perfect knit to keep the man in your life warm. The shawl collar is a really nice detail and not as difficult as it looks!

About this Pattern...

Skills Used

Cables

Working in rows and Rnds

Increasing and decreasing

Pick up and knit

Yarn Alternatives

£   *Save:* Coldharbour Mill DK

££ *Spend:* Debbie Bliss Cashmerino DK

£££ *Treat:* Drops Angora Tweed

Yarn Used

ColourMart 2/6NM DK • 73% merino, 12% Viscose, 10% silk, 5% cashmere • 445m/490yd/150g • WPI 14

Colour: Perla Tweed (grey)

Tension

Work 20 sts and 30 rows to measure 10 x 10cm or 4 x 4in in stocking stitch using 4mm (US 6) needles, or a size needed to obtain tension.

Notions

A 4mm (US 6) circular needle 80cm/32in long

A 3.5 (US 4) circular needle 80cm/32in long

A set of four 4mm (US 6) double-pointed needles

Two cable needles

Stitch markers

A tapestry needle

Special stitch patterns

Pattern A (in the round)

Rnd 1: Knit.

Rep Rnd 1 for patt.

Pattern A (worked flat)

Row 1 (RS): Knit.

Row 2 (WS): Purl.

Pattern B (in the round)

(worked over 1 st)

Rnd 1: Sl 1 with yarn in back.

Rnd 2: Knit.

Rep Rnds 1-2 for patt.

Pattern B (worked flat)

(worked over 1 st)

Row 1 (RS): Sl 1 with yarn in back.

Row 2: P1.

Pattern C (in the round)

(worked over 30 sts)

Rnds 1-4: P2, k6, p2, k10, p2, k6, p2.

Rnd 5: P2, C6B, p2, C10, p2, C6B, p2.

Rnd 6: P2, k6, p2, k10, p2, k6, p2.

Rep Rnds 1-6 for patt.

Pattern C (worked flat)

(worked over 30 sts) Rows 1 and 3 (RS): P2, k6, p2, k10, p2, k6, p2.

Rows 2 and 4: K2, p6, k2, p10, k2, p6, k2.

Row 5: P2, C6B, p2, C10, p2, C6B, p2.

Row 6: K2, p6, k2, p10, k2, p6, k2.

Pattern Notes

Bodice is worked in the round from the hem to the underarm. The sleeves are picked up from the armholes and worked in the round to the cuff.

Special Abbreviations

C6B

Slip 3 sts to cable needle and hold in back, k3, k3 from cable needle.

C10

Slip 4 sts to cable needle and hold in back, slip 2 sts to separate cable needle and hold in front, k4, twist the front cable needle 180-degrees clockwise and knit the 2 sts from cable needle, k4 from back cable needle.

Size & yarn amount

Finished chest	99.5	109	119.5	cm
	39	43	47	in
To fit chest	94	104	114.25	cm
	37	41	45	in
Length	66.25	69.75	72.25	cm
	26½	27½	28½	in
Yarn	4	4	5	balls
Total metres	1500	1600	1800	
Total yards	1633	1796	1959	

Pattern D (worked in the round)

(worked over a multiple of 6 sts)

Rnds 1-2: *P1, k5; rep from * to end of round.

Rnd 3-4: *K1, p1, k3, p1; rep from * to end of round.

Rnd 5-6: *K2, p1, k1, p1, k1; rep from * to end of round.

Rnd 7-8: *K3, p1, k2; rep from * to end of round.

Rnd 9-10: *K2, p1, k1, p1, k1; rep from * to end of round.

Rnd 11-12: *K1, p1, k3, p1; rep from * to end of round.

Rep Rnds 1-12 for pattern.

Pattern D (worked flat)

(worked over a multiple of 6 sts)

Row 1: *P1, k5; rep from * to end of row.

Row 2: *P5, k1; rep from * to end of row.

Row 3: *K1, p1, k3, p1; rep from * to end of row.

Row 4: *K1, p3, k1, p1; rep from * to end of row.

Row 5: *K2, p1, k1, p1, k1; rep from * to end of row.

Row 6: *P1, k1, p1, k1, p2; rep from * to end of row.

Row 7: *K3, p1, k2; rep from * to end of row.

Row 8: *P2, k1, p3; rep from * to end of row.

Row 9: *K2, p1, k1, p1, k1 ; rep from * to end of row.

Row 10: *P1, k1, p1, k1, p2; rep from * to end of row.

Row 11: *K1, p1, k3, p1 ; rep from * to end of row.

Row 12: *K1, p3, k1, p1; rep from * to end of row.

Body

With smaller circular needle, cast on 200 (220, 240) sts. Join, be careful not to twist sts. Place a marker at beg of rnd and after 100 (110, 120) sts to mark side seams.

Work 20 rounds in k2, p2 rib. Switch to larger needles. K1 rnd, increasing 20 sts evenly over round. 220 (240, 260) sts, 110 (120, 130) sts each for front and back.

Next rnd: *Patt A 8 (10,12), patt B 1, patt C 30, patt B 1, patt D 30 (36,42), patt B 1, patt C 30, patt B 1, Patt A 8 (10,12); rep from * once more.

Work in est patt until work measures 45.75 (47, 48.25)cm/18 (18.5, 19)in. Move last 110 (120, 130) sts to holder and work Back section on remaining sts.

Back

Next row (RS): Patt A 8 (10,12), patt B 1, patt C 30, patt B 1, patt D 30 (36,42), patt B 1, patt C 30, patt B 1, Patt A 8 (10,12). Turn.

Work flat in established pattern until piece measures 20.5 (22.75, 24)cm/8.5 (9, 9.5)in from armhole. Total length of piece is 66.25 (69.75, 72.25)cm or 26.5 (27.5, 28.5)in. Move remaining sts of back to holder.

Front

Move Front sts to needle and re-attach yarn. Work flat in established pattern for 12 rows.

Next row (RS): Work 45 (50, 55) sts in est patt, cast off 20 sts, work in est patt to end. Working both sides of neck at the same time and attaching a new ball of yarn to the Left Front Neck

On the following row, cont in patt, decreasing 1 st at neck edge every 6th row 5 (6, 7) times. 40 (44, 48) sts rem for each shoulder after decreases are complete.

Work until piece measures same length to shoulders as Back. Keeping centre 30 (32, 34) sts of neck on holders, join shoulders using three-needle cast off.

Sleeves (make 2)

With DPNs, pick up and knit 94 (102, 106) sts around armhole, starting at the beginning of where the front splits from back. Pm and join to work in the rnd.
Rnd 1: Patt A 31 (35, 37), patt B 1, patt C 30, patt B 1, patt A 31 (35, 37).

Cont in patt, decreasing 1 st at each end of rnd (2 sts dec per rnd) every 6 (4, 4) rnds until 60 sts remain. Work even in patt until sleeve measures 38 (40.5, 43.25)cm/15 (16, 17)in. Work in k2, p2 rib for another 7.5cm/3in.
Cast off all sts.

Shawl collar

With larger circular needle, and making sure that the total number of sts picked up is evenly divisible by 4, pick up and knit 2 sts for every 3 rows up front right neck, knit all held sts from back neck, pick up and knit 2 sts for every 3 rows down front left neck.

Do not join.
Turn.
Work in k2, p2 rib until work measures 11.5cm/4.5in.
Cast off all stitches.

Finishing

Weave in ends.
Sew sides of collar down to centre front neck cast off sts, making sure that the left side of collar overlaps the right side.
Block to measurements.

This yarn feels stiff at first, but it softens greatly when you work with it. There is enough elasticity in it to work cables.

Schematic

66.25 (69.75, 72.25)cm
26.5 (27.5, 28.5)in

99.5 (109, 119.5)cm
39 (43, 47)in

Notions
Circular or double-pointed needles, 2.5 and 3mm Stitch markers Needle to weave in ends, 7 buttons

ADVANCED

About this
Pattern...

Skills Used

Decreasing

Pick up and knit / Pick up and purl

Knitting in the round

Knitting in rows

Working from a chart

Measurements

Small, Middle and Large:

Small: from bottom to shoulder:

58cm/22.8in

from bottom to armpit 38cm/15in

Middle: from bottom to armpit:

40cm/15.7in

from bottom to shoulder: 62cm/24.4in

Large: from bottom to armpit

42cm/16.5in

from bottom to shoulder 66cm/26in

Sleeve length: 50cm/19.6in for all sizes

Yarn Used

ColourMart 2-15mm 100% wool –

770 yards per 150 grams – colour 34

(Navy) You need 2 cones of 150 grams

for each size.

Approx needed:

Small: 875-950m/800-850yd

Middle: 950-985m/850-900yd

Large: 985-1040m/900-950yd

Yarn Alternatives

£ **Save:** Sirdar Calico Cotton

££ **Spend:** Opal Uni

£££ **Treat:** Bristol Yarn Gallery
Buckingham

Buttoned
Cardigan

This wonderful cables-and-seed stitch gives it a
classic look that will look great on any man.

Special stitch patterns

This pattern contains a chart

Pattern notes

Seed stitch:

Row 1: k1: p1 (repeat)

Row 2: knit as sts appear in front of you

Row 3: p1: k1 (repeat)

Row 4: knit as sts appear in front of you

Pattern starts

Lower Body

Cast on With 3.0 mm needles:

220-240-260 sts.

Place markers:

S: 55-110-55

M: 60-120-60

L: 65-130-65

Ribbing:

Work 20 rows in k2 p2 rib.

Continue:

Knit 1 row

Purl 1 row

Divide for pattern

Front left and right

Small: 11 sts A: 34 sts B: 10 sts A

Middle: 13 sts A: 34 sts B: 13 sts A

Large: 16 sts A: 34 sts B: 15 sts A

Cast ON

Front left and right

Small: 11 sts A: 34 sts B: 10 sts A

Middle: 13 sts A: 34 sts B: 13 sts A

Large: 16 sts A: 34 sts B: 15 sts A

For the back

Small: 11 sts A: 34 sts B: 20 sts A: 34 sts B:

11 sts A

Middle: 13 sts A: 34 sts B: 26 sts A: 34 sts

B: 13 sts A

Large: 16 sts A: 34 sts B: 30 sts A: 34 sts

B: 16 sts A

A: Seed stitch

B: Chart over 34 sts

Work in pattern scheme until a length of

38 – 40 – 42cm/15-15.7-16.5in is reached.

From here the parts are knit separate.

Tension

Work 28 st and 36 rows in seed stitch

st to measure 10 x 10cm/4 x 4in using

3mm needles, or size required to

obtain tension.

Right front

Work over the first 55-60-65 sts: (start with right side in front) Work in pattern.
Decrease for V-neck shape:
SSK (stitch 1 and 2) in row 5-11-17 (repeat until total height is reached)
These decreases fall together with the rows in which you need to cable.

Cast off sts when a total length of 58-62-66cm/22.8-24.4-26in is reached.

Back

Work over 110 -120-130 sts: (start with right side in front)Work in pattern.
Cast off sts when a total length of 58-62-66cm/22.8-24.4-26in is reached.

Left front

Work over the remaining 55-60-65 sts, (Start with right side in front).
K2tog the last two sts, in row 5-11-17 (repeat until total height is reached).

These decreases fall together with the rows in which you need to cable.

Cast off sts when a total length of 58-62-66cm/22.8-24.4-26in is reached.

Shoulders

Sew from arm to neck: the first 34-36-39 sts. Secure and weave in ends.

Key

Cable over 6 sts: Place 3 on cable needle in front of your work, knit 3, knit 3 from cable needle.

Cable over 6 sts: Place 3 on cable needle at the back of your work, knit 3, knit 3 from cable needle.

Cable over 4 sts: Place 1st on cable needle at back of your work, knit 3, purl 1 from cable needle.

Cable over 4 sts: Place 3sts on cable needle in front of your work, purl 1, knit 3 from cable needle.

Twist 6 st: Place 6 st on cable needle, twist counter clockwise 180°, knit sts from cable needle.

Cable over 3 sts: Place 2 st on cable needle in front of work, purl 1, knit 2 from cable needle.

Cable over 2 sts: Pace 1 st on cable needle in front of work, purl 1, knit 1 from cable needle.

Cable over 3 sts: Place 1 on cable needle at the back of work, knit 2, purl 1 from cable needle.

Cable over 2 sts: Place 1st on cable needle in front of work, knit1, purl 1 from cable needle.

Sleeves

Worked in the round. Start in armpit – with
needles 3mm, pick up 92-96-100 sts.
Mark the beginning point of your round.
Work in pattern A (seed stitch)
Decrease however in every 10th round: 2 x
1 st repeat these decreases another 7 times
(8 times in total)

Work in the round until a total arm length
of 45 cm is reached. Switch to 2.5 mm
needles.

Ribbing

k2 p2 rib for 5cm/2in. Cast off sts.
Work second sleeve.

Border: Right front

Work in rows:
With right side in front: Pick up sts for
border over a length of 38-40-42cm/
15-15.7-16.5in [direction: bottom
to armpit] (76-80-84 st)
Turn.

Border: Left front

Work in rows: With right side in front:
Pick up sts for border over a length of
38-40-42cm/15-15.7-16.5in [direction:
armpit to bottom]
(76-80-84 st)
Turn.

Work rows in k2, p2 rib: 4 rows
Row 5: k2, p2.

Make button holes: for all sizes:
Sts: 3 + 4, 15 + 16, 27 + 28, 39 + 40,
51 + 52, 63 + 64, p2tog, Yo, Yo.
Row 6: Continue to work in k2, p2 rib –
drop the extra YO.
Row 7 – 10: Work in k2 p 2 rib. Cast off
sts loosely.

Neckline

Start on right front: Pick up sts along the
neckline to the left front. (128 – 136 – 144
st) Turn. Work in k2, p2 rib for 5 rows.
Cast off sts loosely.
Weave in all ends. Sew buttons.

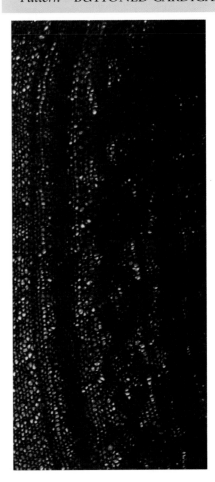

Chart

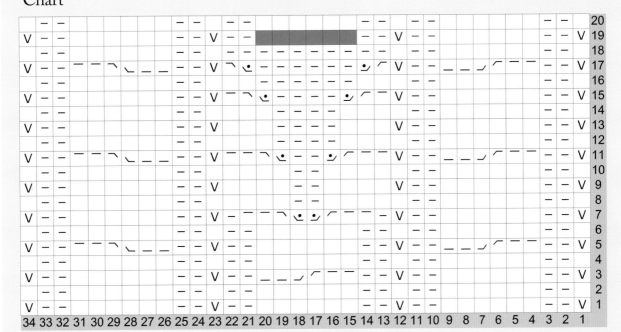

Men's Scarf

This uses super chunky yarn for a quick and cosy hand-knitted scarf.

About this Pattern...

1

BEGINNER

Skills Used
Knit
Cast Off
Fringing

Finished Measurements
300 x 10cm/118 x 4in

Yarn Used
Rowan Big Wool • 100% merino
• 100g/80m/87yd • WPI 6
Colours: Acer, Linen and Lichen

Yarn Alternatives
£   *Save:* Twilleys of Stamford Freedom
££ *Spend:* Cascade Magnum
£££ *Treat:* Sirdar Big Softie

Tension
Work 8 st and 14 rows in Garter st to measure 10 x 10cm/4 x 4in using 9mm (US 13) needles, or size required to obtain tension.

Notions
A 9mm (US 13) circular needle – 80cm/30in or longer

Finishing
Cut one 20cm/8in length of each yarn. Fold in half, pull the folded end through the non-fringed edge of the scarf. Draw the loose tails through the loop and pull tight to secure, creating a matching fringe.

Cast ON

Scarf
With Yarn A, make a slipknot leaving a 10cm/4in tail and cast on 200 stitches and work 2 rows in Garter stitch (knit every row). Cut the yarn at the end to leave a 10cm/4in fringe.
Join Colour B (leaving a 10cm/4in tail) and work 2 rows in Garter st. Cut the yarn at the end to leave a 10cm/4in fringe.
Join Colour C (leaving a 10cm/4in tail) and work 2 rows in Garter st. Cut the yarn at the end to leave a 10cm/4in fringe.

Repeat the previous 6 rows.
Cast off.

Children's

What could be more satisfying to knit than a warm hat for a newborn baby? Create something soft and snugly for a tiny tot with this fun and playful children's section.

3ⁱⁿ1 Baby Hats

Who can resist knitting baby hats? Small and fast to knit, treat them as a handy swatch for a new stitch.

M ost non-knitters see baby items as the one thing they wished they could knit. There is something so satisfying about knitting tiny garments for newborn babies – it's a great way to show that you care and give a hand-made gift without investing a great deal of time or money. It is also a good way to experiment with new stitches, yarns or techniques – if it doesn't work out you can start again easily. The three hat patterns suggested here are a blank canvas – change the number of stitches cast on and rows knitted and you'll have a hat that is suitable for a slightly larger or smaller baby. Babies come in all shapes and sizes, so these will fit a baby of between 1 and 3

Pattern 1: Cabled hat

Using Rooster Almerino DK and 4mm needles, cast on 80 stitches and work 6 rows in 1x1 rib.

Cast ON

Begin cables

Row 1: P2, K6, rep to end.
Row 2: K2, P6, rep to end.
Row 3: P2, C3F, P2, K6, rpt to end.
Row 4: K2, P6, rep to end.
Row 5: P2, K6, rep to end.
Row 6: K2, P6, rep to end.
Row 7: P2, K6, rep to end.
Row 8: K2, P6, rep to end.
Row 9: P2, K6, P2, C3F, rep to end.
Repeat these 9 rows twice more, ending with row 7. Next row: K2, P6, rep to end.

Decrease for the crown

Row 1: P2, K6, P2, K2, K2tog, K2, rep to end – decrease every other column.
Row 2: K2, P5, K2, P6, rep to end – work stitches as set.
Row 3: P2, C3F, P2, K5, rep to end – cable row, no decreases.
Row 4: K2, P5, K2, P6, rep to end – work stitches as set.
Row 5: P2, K2, K2tog, K2, P2, K1, K2tog, K2, rep to end – decreasing every column.
Row 6: K2, P6, rep to end – work stitches as set.
Row 7: P2, K1, K2tog, K2, P2, K4, rep to end – decreasing every other column.
Row 8: K2, P4, rep to end – work stitches as set.
Row 9: P2, K4, P2, C2F, rep to end – cable row, no decreases.
Row 10: K2, P4, rep to end – work stitches as set.
Row 11: P2, K4, P2, K2tog, K2, rep to end – decrease every other column.
Row 12: K2, P3, K2, P4, rep to end – work stitches as set.
Row 13: P2, C2F, P2, K3, rep to end – cable row, no decreases.
Row 14: K2, P3, K2, P3 – work stitches as set.
Row 15: P2, K3tog, rep to end – decrease every column.
Row 16: K2, P2, rep to end – work stitches as set.
Row 17: P2tog, K2tog to end.
Break yarn and draw through stitches, seam the side.

Special Stitch Patterns

C3F (cable 3 front) as follows:
Slip next 3 sts onto cable needle and
hold at front of work, knit next 3 sts,
knit 3 sts from cable needle.
C2F (cable 2 front) as follows: Slip next 2 sts
onto cable needle and hold at front of work,
knit next 2 sts, knit 2 sts from cable needle.
Feather-and-Fan stitch, worked over 18 stitches:
Row 1: K2tog 3 times, K1, YO 6 times,
K2tog 3 times (rep to end)
Row 2: Purl

Pattern 2: Striped hat

Cast ON

Using 4mm needles and Rowan
Felted Tweed, cast on 70 stitches
and work in a 4-row striped pattern for 36 rows.

Crown decreases

Keeping the stripe pattern constant,
decrease as follows:

Row 1: K6, K2 tog, rep to end.

Row 2 and each alternate row: Purl.

Row 3: K5, K2tog, rep to end.

Row 5: K4, K2tog, rep to end.

Row 7: K3, K2tog, rep to end.

Row 9: K2, K2tog, rep to end.

Row 11: K1, K2tog, rep to end.

Row 13: K2tog, rep to end.

Break yarn and draw through stitches,
seam the side and allow brim to curl.

*These patterns are infinitely adaptable and accommodate
any level of new stitch you want to experiment with!*

Pattern 3: Lace hat

Cast ON

Using DK yarn and 4mm needles, cast on
72 stitches. Work in Feather-and-Fan stitch,
as described, for a total of 20 rows.

Begin crown decreases

Row 1: K2tog 3 times, K1, YO 6 times,
K2tog 3 times (rep to end).

Row 2: Purl.

Row 3: K2tog 3 times, K3, YO, K3 , K2tog 3 times
(rep to end).

Row 4: Purl.

Row 5: K2tog 2 times, K2, YO, K2, K2tog 2 times
(rep to end).

Row 6: Purl.

Row 7: K2 tog, K1, YO, K1, K2tog.

Row 8: Purl.

Row 9: K2tog, YO, K2tog.

Row 10: Purl.

Break yarn and draw through stitches, seam the side.

About this Pattern...

Yarn Used

Sublime, Organic Merino Wool DK, 100% organic merino.

Yarn Alternatives

£ *Save:* Acrylic yarns oddments

££ *Spend:* Wool yarn oddments

£££ *Treat:* Cashmere yarn oddments

Tension

Work 22 sts and 30 rows to measure 10 x 10cm/4 x 4in in st st using 4mm (US6).

Notions

4mm (US6) straight needles or size needed to obtain tension

Pattern Notes

Stripe sequence (back)

Shade A: 118

Shade B: 114

Shade C: 112

Shade D: 117

Stripe sequence (front)

Shade A: 118

Shade B: 114

Shade C: 117

Number of rows per stripe

Age 2: 4 rows, Age 3: 6 rows, Age 4: 8 rows, Age 5: 10 rows.

When changing colours, work the first row of the new colour in purl to create the bumped edge in between the stripes. You will then work the next row in purl to get back into st st.

Boys' Tank Top

This boys' tank is a great way to use up single skeins of yarn. For added interest, use slightly different stripe patterns on the back and front.

Pattern starts: Back

Using shade A, cast on 56 (58, 60, 62) sts.

Work in st st for a further 10 rows ending with a WS row before changing colour for the first time.

Changing colour as shown on the patten notes, work 7 stripes in pattern

Change yarn for 8th stripe and p next 2 rows.

Cast ON

Shape armholes

Cast off 2 stitches at the beginning of the next 2 rows to shape the armholes.

Continue in st st until piece measures 31 (36, 41, 46)cm/12 (14, 16, 18)in.

Cast off all sts.

Pattern Note

This tank is designed with raw edges for a rolled, natural look.

Front

Work as for back until 6 rows after armhole shaping, ending with a WS row.

Shape neck

k to middle of row, turn and p to end.
Next row (RS) k to last 3 sts,
k2tog, k1.
Next row (WS) p to end.
Repeat last 2 rows until 12 sts remain.
Continue in st st until piece measures
31 (36, 41, 46)cm/12 (14, 16, 18)in.
Cast off all sts.
Rejoin yarn to other side of front.
Next row k to end.
Next row p to end.
Next row k1, ssk, k to end.
Next row p to end.
Repeat last 2 rows until 12 sts remain.
Continue in st st until piece measures
12 (14, 16, 18)in, 31 (36, 41, 46)cm
Cast off all sts.

Finishing

Weave in ends. Sew front and back together. Block if desired.

Size and yarn guide

Age	2	3	4	5	
Actual chest measurement	20	21	21.5	22	in
	51	53	55	56	cm
Length	12	14	16	18	in
	31	36	41	46	cm
Sublime, Organic Merino, 50g/105m/113yd 112 114 117 118	1 ball each	1 ball each	1 ball each	1 ball each	
Total meters	420	420	420	420	
Total yards	452	452	452	452	

1
BEGINNER

Girls' Striped
Cardigan

This cool cardigan would make a lovely addition to
any girl's wardrobe, its nautical style appealing to
little tomboys and budding fashionistas alike.

Body

Cast ON

Cast on 138 (158, 168, 188) sts.
PM after 34 (40, 42, 47) sts and
104 (118, 126, 141) sts to mark side
'seams.' Begin stripe pattern and work in st
st throughout. Continue in stocking stitch
until work measures 14 (15.25, 16.5, 17.75)
cm/5.5 (6, 6.5, 7)in, ending with a WS row.
Work eyelet row: K0 (0, 2, 2), (K2, yo,
k2tog) to last 2 (2, 4, 4) sts, k2 (2, 4, 4).
Purl 1 row.
Continuing in st st and with the stripe
pattern as set, shape front edge by working
the decrease row on the next and following
fourth row 10 times as follows:
Decrease row: K2, k2tog, k to last 4 sts,
k2togtbl, k2.
116 (136, 146, 166) sts remain. 23 (29, 31,
36) sts before first marker and after third
marker.
Work even in patt until work measures 30.5
(33, 35.5, 38)cm/12 (13, 14, 15)in ending
with a WS row. Shape armholes by splitting
work as follows.

Right front

Knit to first marker, remove marker and turn
and work on these stitches.
Cast off 3 stitches at beginning of row and
then work even in st st and stripe patt until
armhole measures, 5 (6.5, 7.5, 7.5)cm/2 (2,
3, 3)in ending with a WS row. 20 (26, 28,
33) sts.

Leave sts on a holder and rejoin yarn to
main piece of work at Back with RS facing.

Back

Cast off 3 sts, k to next marker.
Remove marker and turn and work on
these sts.
Cast off 3 stitches at beg of next row.
66 (72, 78, 88) sts.
Continue in st st and working stripe pattern
as set until work measures 5 (6.5, 7.5, 7.5)
cm/2 (2.5, 3, 3)in, ending with a WS row.
Leave stitches on a holder and rejoin yarn to
main piece of work.

Left front

Cast off 3 stitches and knit to end.
Continue to work in st st and stripe patt, until armhole measures 5 (6.5, 7.5, 7.5) cm/2 (2½, 3, 3)in ending with a WS row. 20 (26, 28, 33) sts.

Shape raglan

Turn and purl across Left Front, PM, cast on 17 (19, 21, 23) sts for sleeve, PM, purl across Back sts, PM, cast on 17 (19, 21, 23) sts for sleeve, PM, purl across Right Front. 140 (162, 176, 200) sts.
Shape Raglan, cont in stripe patt as follows:
Next row (RS): *K to 2 sts before m, k2tog, sm, k2tog; rep from * three times more, k to end.
Next row (WS): *P to 2 sts before m, p2tog, sm, p2tog; rep from * three times

more, p to end.
Rep last 2 rows 6 (7, 8, 9) times more. 28 (34, 32, 40) sts rem.
Next row (RS): *K to 2 sts before m, ssk, sm, k3tog, sm, k2tog; rep from * once more, k to end. 20 (26, 22, 32) sts rem.
Work even until the next stripe of colour is completed and cast off all sts.

Finishing

Pick up and knit 3 sts for every 4 rows along the left edge and then cast off without knitting a row.
Repeat for other side and around armholes.
Cut 2 lengths of yarn (one in each colour) that are approx 2m/2yd long. Twist to make a 2-colour cord and thread through the eyelets to fasten.

Schematic

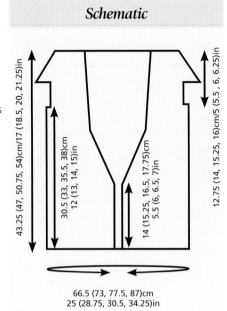

43.25 (47, 50.75, 54)cm/17 (18.5, 20, 21.25)in

30.5 (33, 35.5, 38)cm
12 (13, 14, 15)in

14 (15.25, 16.5, 17.75)cm
5.5 (6, 6.5, 7)in

12.75 (14, 15.25, 16)cm/5 (5.5, 6, 6.25)in

66.5 (73, 77.5, 87)cm
25 (28.75, 30.5, 34.25)in

The fresh nautical stripes and luscious cotton-blend yarn give this cardigan a classic, timeless feel.

Size and yarn amount

Age	7-8	9-10	11-12	13-14	years
Finished chest	25	28½	30½	34	in
	66	72	78	87	cm
Length	17	18½	20	21¼	in
	43.25	47	50.75	54	cm
Yarn (MC) balls	3	4	4	5	
Total metres	360	480	480	600	
Total yards	393	524	524	655	
Yarn (CC) balls	3	4	4	5	
Total metres	360	480	480	600	
Total yards	393	524	524	655	

Pattern Notes

The bottom of this cardigan is supposed to roll organically – if you would prefer for this to be more structured, you should work 4 rows of garter stitch before beginning the pattern as set.

Rainbow Legwarmers

Quick to knit and fun to wear these legwarmers are a good basic project for beginners.

Pattern starts

Cast ON

Cast on 44 stitches using solid yarn and join to work in round.
Work in 2 x 2 rib for 10 rounds
Continue in stocking stitch for 60 rounds.
Work in 2 x 2 rib for 10 rounds. Cast off.

Finishing

Make second legwarmer in the same way.

About this Pattern...

1
BEGINNER

Skills Used
Knitting in the round

Yarns Used
Oddments of aran weight yarn in different colours.
You will need approx 50g for each pair of legwarmers

Tension
18 stitches and 24 rows to 10cm/4in over stocking stitch using 4.5mm needles

Notions
4.5mm DPNs or circulars
Darning needle

Little Shrug

This pretty little lace shrug is the perfect way to use up a little bit of very lovely yarn.

Pattern Notes

The pattern is easy to make longer if you have more yarn – simply increase the lace section for the arms.

Cast ON

Pattern starts: Sleeve 1

Cast on 57 (57, 63, 63, 67, 67, 73, 73, 79, 79) stitches and work 4 rows in garter stitch.

*Row 1 (RS): (K2tog, yo) to last st, k1.
Row 2: Purl.
Rep last 2 rows 35 (35, 43, 43, 49, 49, 57, 57, 63, 63) times more.**

Back

Work 92 (100, 104,108,112, 118, 120, 126, 138, 148) rows in st st.

Sleeve 2

Rep from * to ** for second sleeve.
Work 4 more rows in garter st.
Cast off.

Finishing

Sew up sleeve seams.
Press and block to measurements.

About this Pattern...

Skills Used

Stocking stitch
Garter stitch
Yarn forward

Yarns Used

Jamie Possum Possum Paint
4 ply, 80% merino 20% possum,
50g/180m/200yd, WPI 14
1 skein (shown in a special
one-off colour)

Yarn Alternatives

£   **Save:** Patons Diploma Gold 4 ply

££ **Spend:** Sublime Extra Fine Merino
Wool 4 ply

£££ **Treat:** Fyberspates Scrumptious

Tension

Work 28 sts and 36 rows to measure 10 x 10cm/4 x 4in in stocking stitch.

Notions

A pair of 3.25mm (US 3) needles
Tapestry needle

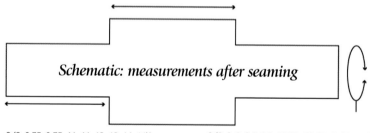

10 (11, 11.5, 12, 12.5, 13, 13.25, 14, 15.25, 16.5)in
25.5 (28, 29.25, 30.5, 31.75, 33, 33.75, 35.5, 38.75, 42)cm

Schematic: measurements after seaming

8 (8, 9.75, 9.75, 11, 11, 13, 13, 14, 14)in
20.5 (20.5, 24.75, 24.75, 28, 28, 33, 33, 35.5, 35.5)cm

8 (8, 9, 9, 9.5, 9.5, 10.25, 10.25, 11.25, 11.25)in
20.5 (20.5, 23, 23, 24, 24, 26, 26, 28.5, 28.5)cm

Size and yarn amount

To fit age	1	2	3	4	5	6	7	8	9	10	years
To fit chest	18.5	20	21	22	23	24	25	26	28.5	30	in
	47	51	54	56	58	61	63	66	72	78	cm
Length	17	18	20	20.5	22.5	23	25	25.5	28.5	29.5	in
	43.5	45.5	51	52	57	58.5	63.5	65	72	75	cm

Baby Dress

2

INTERMEDIATE

This sweet little dress would make the perfect gift for a newborn baby girl. Adjust the size of the pattern for a comfortable fit.

Special Notes

M1: Make 1 st by knitting into the back loop

Cast ON

Pattern Starts

For size 1: 84 sts, distributing them over the four needles as follows: 16-26-16-26

For size 2: 92 sts, distributing them over the four needles as follows: 18-28-18-28

For size 3: 100 sts, distributing them over the four needles as follows: 20-30-20-30

Join in the round, be careful not to twist sts. Place markers to separate the four sections of stitches.

Rnd 1: knit all sts

Rnd 2: purl all sts

Rnd 3: *k1, m1, k to 1 st before marker, m1, k1. Repeat from * to end of round

Rnd 4: purl all sts

Rnds 5 & 7: Repeat Rnd 3

Rnds 6 & 8: Repeat Rnd 1

Rnds 9-14: Repeat Rnd 3-8

Rnds 15: Purl all sts

The stitch count should be:

Size 1: Needle 1 & 3: 28sts;
Needle 2 & 4: 38sts

Size 2: Needle 1 & 3: 30sts;
Needle 2 & 4: 40sts

Size 3: Needle 1& 3: 32sts;
Needle 2 & 4: 42sts

Rnd 16: For needles 1 & 3 cast off, using the following method:

k1, *yo, psso, yo, psso, k1, psso, repeat from *, pass the last sts from that needle over the first sts from needle 2 (or 4) to keep stitch count.

For needles 2 & 4: knit sts

Rnd 17:

Size 1: Needles 1 & 3: cast on 16sts;
Needle 2 & 4: knit all sts

Size 2: Needles 1 & 3: cast on 18sts;
Needle 2 & 4: knit all sts

Size 3: Needles 1 & 3: cast on 21sts;
Needle 2 & 4: knit all sts

Rnd 18: Purl all sts

About this Pattern...

Skills Used

Increasing
Knitting in the round
Basic crochet

Measurements

(Measured flat)

Size 1: Total length from shoulder to bottom skirt: 32cm/12.5in
Width 18cm/7in

Size 2: Total length from shoulder to bottom skirt: 35cm/14in
Width 20cm/8in

Size 3: Total length from shoulder to bottom skirt: 38cm/15in
Width 22cm/9in

Yarns Used

Colinette Jitterbug 100% merino 150g/366m/400yds 14 WPI
Colour: Elephant's Dream (166)
1 skein

Tension

Work 26st and 30 rows in pattern st to measure 10 x 10cm/4 x4in using 3.5mm needles, or size required to obtain tension. These measurements are blocked measurements.

Notions

Long double-pointed needles (one set of five needles, 40cm in length) or circular needles, size 3.5mm
Stitch markers
3mm crochet hook

Yarn Alternatives

£ *Save:* Auracania Ranco Multi

££ *Spend:* John Arbon UK
Alpaca Sock

£££ *Treat:* Fivemoons 4 ply

Skirt pattern

Rnds 1 & 2: k1, sl1 as if to knit, k1.
Repeat around.
Rnds 3 & 4: knit all sts.
Work Rnds 1-4 until 80 (88: 92) rnds
are complete.
Cast off sts.

Sleeve edges

Start in the armpit, by joining the yarn.
1ch, 1dc in every stitch towards the
'corner', (dc2tog twice) Continue working
in the cast off edge: 2dc in every loop from
the cast off edge, towards the corner.

(dc2tog twice), 1dc in every st to complete
the round. Close round with slip stitch.
Fasten off, weave in ends.
Now repeat this process for the
second sleeve.

Neck

Start at the back of the dress. Join yarn,
1ch. *work 1dc in every st towards the
corner. At the corner, dc2tog twice. Repeat
this from* around until you are back at the
beginning point. Fasten off, weave in ends.
Block skirt lightly.